Gaye Nease

THE DEATH PENALTY DEBATE

THE DEATH PENALTY DEBATE

H. Wayne House & John Howard Yoder

WORD PUBLISHING
Dallas·London·Vancouver·Melbourne

THE DEATH PENALTY DEBATE
Issues of Christian Conscience

Library of Congress Cataloging-in-Publication Data
House, H. Wayne
    The death penalty debate: two opposing views of capital punishment / H. Wayne House and John Howard Yoder.
        p.   cm. — (Issues of Christian conscience)
    Includes bibliographical references and index.
    ISBN 0-8499-3307-2
    1. Capital punishment—Religious aspects—Christianity
2. Capital punishment—Biblical teaching.   3. Capital punishment—United States—Moral and ethical aspects.   I. Yoder, John Howard.   II. Title.   III. Series.
HV8694.H68   1991
364.6'6'0973—dc20   91-16811
                                                                          CIP

Printed in the United States of America
1 2 3 4 9 RRD 9 8 7 6 5 4 3 2 1

Contents

v

Foreword

For Christians who believe that God's image has been imprinted on every member of our *homo sapiens* species, the deliberate termination of a human life presents awesome ethical problems. The stringent prohibition of the Decalog's sixth commandment, "You shall not kill," applies, it is agreed, to murder. But does that law also apply on the battlefield and in the gas chamber? If the government of some country legitimizes killing in war or the execution of a murderer, is the sixth commandment being violated? When, if ever, and by what authority, if any, can life be taken? Have both Israelites and Christians tragically misunderstood God's will regarding this issue as set forth in Scripture? Equally pious and scholarly individuals have disagreed radically concerning the right answer to these questions. That disagreement persists today.

Proponents of capital punishment, who as a rule are likewise committed to the "just war" position, argue that today as perhaps never before the proper interpretation of this commandment is imperative. For example, Iraq's violent seizure of Kuwait in 1990 was the catalyst for fierce conflict in the Persian Gulf. An international coalition of nations, avowing the justice of its intervention, became engaged in driving the forces of Saddam Hussein out of that sheikdom. The cost in terms of death and destruction was worse than appalling. While regretting the carnage involved, policy makers such as President Bush contended that war-time killing, even collaterally of civilians, is not murder. It is using the sword morally with biblical sanction.

As for putting murderers to death, that judicial killing—so proponents of capital punishment contend—does more than fulfill the edict of Genesis 9:6, "'Whoever sheds the blood of man, by man shall his blood be shed; for in the image of God has God made man'" (NIV). It acts likewise as an effective deterrent to similar crimes. And in our late twentieth-century society with its sickening increase of homicide, deterrence is sorely needed. Biblically mandated, then, legalized executions in no way contradict God's ban on killing as a personal act which is heinous in nature.

But opponents of capital punishment maintain that appeals to Scripture in support of government-decreed killing are hermeneutically indefensible. Rightly understood, Scripture gives no divine endorsement to the killing of even killers. More than that, life ending by legitimized life takers does not deter murder; it brutalizes society, denying in practice the incalculable value which is theoretically imputed to every human being.

Drs. House and Yoder are able spokespersons for their respective convictions regarding capital punishment. Dr. House espouses it; Dr. Yoder is set against it. Each respects the other's stance while criticizing his exegesis and logic. The reader must therefore judge for himself or herself whose argument is more persuasive and biblical. Hopefully, though, this dialogue will enable Christians to move beyond mere irrational emotionalism to a revelational, reasoned, and relevant perspective on this literally life-and-death issue.

VERNON GROUNDS

In Favor of the Death Penalty
H. Wayne House

1

Issues and Different Positions on Capital Punishment

The morning newspaper reports yet another incident of the brutal murder of a young child, and the reader reacts in horror and anger, and senses an intense longing for immediate revenge. Then he opens his Bible and reads, "Thou shalt not kill." Again he winces, apparently caught on the horns of a dilemma. To many, the death penalty seems an obvious payment for such a heinous crime, but can a Christian support capital punishment? Does the Bible permit the death penalty? Supporters and opponents of capital punishment both claim that theirs is the true Christian position, but both cannot be right. Is capital punishment biblically mandated or not?

Tension over capital punishment runs high in today's society, fueled in part by the rapidly increasing national crime rate. According to a 1985 study, a "murder takes place every twenty-three minutes, a rape every six minutes, a robbery every fifty-five seconds, and a motor vehicle theft every twenty-nine seconds."[1] Some argue that this increase is directly related to the decrease in executions, for there has been a trend toward fewer and fewer executions for capital crimes as the following table demonstrates:[2]

Years	Number of Executions
1935–1939	891
1940–1944	645
1945–1949	639
1950–1954	413
1955–1959	304
1960–1965	181
1966–1969	10
1970–1975	0
1976–1979	1
1980–1981	1

Yet, in spite of the rising crime rate, many argue for abolition of the death penalty, claiming that it is incompatible with the evolutionary improvement of moral nature. Others, however, support capital punishment, pragmatically arguing that severe penalties help deter crime and motivate criminals to reform. The serious Christian, however, must evaluate the issue from the unique perspective of being "under the law of Christ" (1 Cor. 9:21). Believers are citizens who live under the authority of the state and share civic responsibility for shaping that authority through their votes. We also live under the ultimate authority of God's Word, so for us the ultimate question is not sociological or psychological, but theological: What has God said about capital punishment? If God has clearly spoken on this issue, and we believe that he has, then his word is the final answer for the believer. Our purpose in this discussion, then, is to find that answer.

Discussions over the topic have often been passionate and heated, both in and out of the church. Pierre Viansson-Ponté put it well when he said,

> Hardly any other question gives rise to such intense passions and so many firm judgments as does capital punishment. Men and women usually would hesitate to express themselves so confidently about other topics.[3]

Advocates of both sides lobby legislators, hold rallies, and claim to have the ultimate truth on the matter. In the process they often lose proper perspective, frequently lowering themselves to jeers or snide remarks against those who differ, or attributing false motives to opponents. Julia Johnsen, for example, argues that since Jesus taught that forgiveness is the greatest of Christian virtues, no Christian can "advocate capital punishment and be true to his faith."[4]

Supporters of the death penalty are also guilty of overstatement, so much so that David Llewellyn, in an article entitled "The Sobering Horror," admonishes proponents of capital punishment against undue enthusiasm in their support of executions:

> "Christians" have sometimes been known to advocate the death penalty with an ardor approaching glee. Such enthusiasm is shameful. With our compassionate Creator we should declare, "As I live, I take not pleasure in the death of the wicked, but that the wicked turn from their ways and live" (Ezek. 33:11).[5]

These same passions have been rekindled through history, for today's debate over capital punishment is nothing new. The death penalty has been argued for centuries. The American aspect of the debate finds its roots in England before this country became a nation. For example, a paper presented before the English House of Parliament in 1701 argued that "those who show no mercy should find none." However, this opinion was not shared by all in America. In a paper written in 1872, Horace Greeley stated that "it is a sorrowful mistake and barbarity to do any such thing."[6]

Even the Christian community has been divided over this question since the early days of the church, though those who oppose all capital punishment have been in the clear minority. Historically, leaders of the church have supported capital punishment. Martin Luther, for example, claimed that

> neither God nor government was included in this [fifth, Lutheran reckoning] commandment ("Thou shalt not kill"). Their right to take human life is not abrogated. God has delegated His authority of punishing evildoers to civil magistrates.[7]

Opinion within the mainline denominations began to shift, as men like Schleiermacher in the nineteenth century and Karl Barth in the twentieth raised their voices against capital punishment. Barth argued that in the crucifixion of Christ God "took the instrument of death as a punishment out of human hands. . . . Since Christ, therefore, the only form of human punishment is educative and resocializing measures."[8]

Today, most mainline denominations reject capital punishment as un-Christian. Leaders as diverse as Pope John Paul II and Charles Colson agree in their opposition to death as punishment. Perhaps their arguments are best summarized in a 1960 American Baptist resolution:

> Because the Christian believes in the inherent worth of human personality and in the unceasing availability of God's mercy, forgiveness, and redemptive power, and
> Because the Christian wholeheartedly supports the emphasis in modern penology upon the process of creative, redemptive rehabilitation rather than on punishment and primitive retribution, and
> Because the deterrent effects of capital punishment are not supported by available evidence, and
> Because the death penalty tends to brutalize the human spirit and the society which condones it, and
> Because human agencies of legal justice are fallible, permitting the possibility of the executing of the innocent,
> We, therefore, recommend the abolition of capital punishment and the re-evaluation of the parole system relative to such cases.[9]

Our discussion of capital punishment addresses the points raised by this resolution. We will consider issues of law, sociology, and psychology, but the center of our argument is the Bible and its teachings on capital punishment with a concern for contemporary application. But, as with any question of historical significance, proposed answers must be evaluated in light of that history. Our discussion, therefore, begins with a brief survey of the history of capital punishment.

The History of Capital Punishment

The death penalty has existed in some form throughout almost all of recorded history, the most common forms being decapitation and hanging. Imperial Rome crucified thieves and slaves outside the Eternal City. Being hurled alive from the Tarpeian Rock was the penalty in Rome itself, along with being fed to wild animals in the Coliseum. Japan employed crucifixion until the nineteenth century. In medieval Europe criminals of low social degree were hanged while nobles were decapitated. The English penalty of "drawing and quartering" was especially brutal. "The victim was first partly strangled and then while still alive drawn or disemboweled, his entrails were burned and his body then literally butchered into four pieces."[10] The French pulled traitors apart with draft horses or crushed the guilty by tying them to large wheels.

Usually these executions were public spectacles, but in the mid-nineteenth century opinion turned against such displays. Consequently, after 1868 most executions in England were done in private, usually in prisons. In the twentieth century, opinion turned against the death penalty itself and in 1965 England abolished capital punishment altogether.

The legal situation in the United States is somewhat different from that of England, for here the matter of capital punishment is primarily a matter of state law. Such laws, however, must conform to the Federal Constitution, so they are subject to review by the Supreme Court of the United States. The two most common challenges to the death penalty are based on the Eighth Amendment, which prohibits cruel and unusual punishment, and the Fifth and Fourteenth Amendments which require equal protection under the law for all citizens. During the 1960s, executions ceased while the constitutionality of the death penalty was debated. Finally, in 1972, the Supreme Court ruled that capital punishment was constitutional, but its method of application in many states was not. Consequently, many states rewrote their capital punishment laws to conform to the Court's guidelines and, beginning in 1977, executions again took place. Today there is growing opposition to the death penalty, even though surveys show that a majority of Americans support it. Unfortunately, few of those entering the debate are aware of all the issues surrounding capital punishment.

Issues in the Capital Punishment Debate

The debate over capital punishment contains a host of issues, including definition, recipients, means, and motivation. First of all, what is capital punishment? Mob violence, lynchings, or personal revenge

7

are not capital punishment per se. Instead, *capital punishment is the punishment by death for a specific crime by a duly constituted government following properly enacted laws.*[11] The term *capital punishment* is taken from the Latin *caput*, a word used by the Romans to mean the head, the life, or the civil rights of an individual.[12]

A second question is this: Who should be put to death and for what crime? Our primary concern is with one who has committed murder. By "murder" we refer to the premeditated taking of a person's life by another. Usually this is designated as first-degree murder to distinguish it from other acts of killing where no premeditation is involved, such as crimes of passion, insanity, or accident. There are many who would call for the execution of individuals who commit such crimes as treason and rape as well as murder, but those issues will have to be examined at another time.

A third problem regards the form execution might take. Does execution include physical or even mental torture? Should executions be public or private? Throughout history men have used various methods, both public and private, to execute criminals. The victims have been hanged, burned, boiled in oil, thrown to wild beasts, flayed, drowned, crushed, crucified, stoned, impaled, strangled, torn apart, beheaded, smothered, disemboweled, shot, gassed, or electrocuted. While these questions are important, they will be addressed when we discuss the reason for capital punishment.

Different Motives for Capital Punishment

Supporters of capital punishment usually put forward one of four basic reasons for the death penalty: deterrence of crime, rehabilitation of other criminals, protection of society, and retribution.

Deterrence of Crime—Those who employ this argument distinguish between general and individual deterrence. The concept of general deterrence is not concerned with the future behavior of the criminal, but with the effects of his or her punishment on society as a whole. Criminal laws and punishments make examples of criminals to keep other people from harming society through criminal acts.

Individual deterrence is aimed at the particular criminal. The object of punishment is to teach the offender not to repeat his criminal acts.

Since the more serious crimes are the ones that society would most like to deter, it follows that they warrant greater punishment. If a person knows that his or her criminal actions will be punished, that person is less likely to commit a crime. Its supporters argue that capital punishment accomplishes both goals. As the ultimate punishment for the most severe crime(s), it provides the strongest possible reason for people to choose not to become criminals. On the individual level, execution prevents the criminal from committing further crimes. This is important, since recidivism is a major problem in contemporary society.

Protection of Society—Some argue that the basis for punishment of criminal acts is not retribution or deterrence, but the protection of society. Supporters of this concept argue that criminals should be treated, usually without their consent, by medical means or social retraining in order to eliminate any future problems when they are returned to society. If treatment is not possible, then they should be isolated by a preventive sentence, such as life imprisonment. Capital punishment provides the ultimate protection of society from the criminal by removing him or her from society with no possibility of return.

Rehabilitation—Neither the deterrence view nor the protection concept stresses the rehabilitation of the criminal. They do not ignore this aspect but it is not their chief end. Many today, however, argue that the chief end of criminal law should be the rehabilitation of the criminal. The Model Penal Code proposed by the American Law Institute in 1962, for example, stated that an objective of criminal law should be "to promote the correction and rehabilitation of offenders."[13] Indeed the term *penitentiary* indicates that jails were to be places for the criminal to repent of his or her crime(s). The possibility of capital punishment, the argument goes, provides a strong motivation for those who have not yet committed a capital crime to reform their ways and avoid the death penalty.

Retribution—Punishment is viewed as something that an individual earns by his or her behavior. A society defines acceptable behavior and the punishments accorded nonacceptable conduct. When a person breaks the law, then that punishment is inflicted as prescribed by the law. The punishment fits the crime, i.e., is proportional to the severity of the act, and is limited to the individual committing the crime. Family and friends are not punished for the deeds of another responsible individual. While this concept of punishment may result in deterrence of crime and may lead to the reform of the criminal, these ends are not its primary focus. Retributive punishment is meted out as the necessary return for a specific act.

Theonomic or Reconstructionist View—This view of capital punishment, based on the rule of God through the Mosaic code, shares a perspective of the nature of punishment and justice that is similar to the retributive position. Those holding this position believe that the penalties connected to various crimes/sins in the Law given by Yahweh to Moses should be enforced in all societies, including contemporary Western culture, not just Israel. This view is gaining in popularity, so we will consider it more closely.

Theonomists advance a number of reasons for extending the Old Testament Law to contemporary society: (1) God's Law reflects his unchanging character (2) the New Testament repeats the Ten Commandments, (3) the Old Testament was the Bible of the early church, and (4) Jesus said that he did not come to abolish the Law. Consequently they identify twenty-one different capital crimes, some of which are decidedly cultural in nature, such as breaking the Sabbath (Exod. 31:14), drunken priests on duty (Lev. 10:8–11), and nonpriests touching the holy furniture in the tabernacle (Num. 4:15).

There are, however, important reasons for recognizing that the Mosaic Law is no longer in effect for either the church or society in general. First of all, the New Testament does not repeat all of the Ten Commandments, e.g., the Sabbath command. In point of fact, the early church met on Sunday for worship, something which required travel and work, both of which were proscribed activities for the Sabbath, forbidden in the Old Testament. Next, the New Testament does not apply the Old Testament penalties to sins which were capital offenses under the Law. Paul discussed a case of incest within the Corinthian congregation (1 Cor. 5:1–5), and he ordered the congregation to excommunicate, not execute. While Jesus did not do away with the Law, according to Paul, it was lifted as the rule of life for God's people (Gal. 3:25, Rom. 6:15). Theonomists have a cogent argument for punishment, as we will see in the next chapter, but their foundational concept of the extension of the Mosaic Law to our society must be rejected.[14]

Summary

We have seen that the issue of capital punishment is an important one that demands our attention as Christians. People's lives—those of criminals, and future victims—hang in the balance. Good people differ on the conclusion but this should not cause us to enter into uncharitable debate because of the gravity of the problem. It is our opinion that the biblical and moral basis for belief and practice of capital punishment is very strong and that rejection of this view can only come by adoption (even if unintentionally) of a humanistic mindset and a very selective use of the Scripture.

The procedure for most of the study in our presentation on behalf of capital punishment will be to give a positive presentation for the pro-capital punishment view. At times we will also include an interaction more specifically with certain arguments against the pro position.

NOTES

1. David Woehr, "Prisons," *Faith for the Family* (January 1985): 6.
2. Franklin E. Zimring and Gordon Hawkins, *Capital Punishment and the American Agenda*, p. 5, see bibliography; Karl Spence, "Criminal Punishment," *National Review* (Sept. 16, 1983): 1144.
3. Pierre Viansson-Ponté, "The Call for the Death Penalty," *The Death Penalty and Torture*, eds. Franz Böckle and Jacques Pohier (New York: Seabury Press, 1979), 86.
4. Julia E. Johnsen, ed., *Capital Punishment* (New York: H. W. Wilson, 1939), 83.
5. David Llewellyn, "The Sobering Horror: Reconsidering Old Testament's Support for the Modern Application of the Death Penalty," *The Other Side* 132 (Sept. 1982): 13–15.
6. Horace Greeley, "The Death Penalty Is State Sanctioned Murder, 1872," *The Death Penalty: Opposing Viewpoints*, eds. David L. Bender and Bruno Leone (St. Paul: Greenhaven Press, 1986), 38.
7. Quoted in "The Capital Punishment Debate," The Standing Committee for Church in Society, American Lutheran Church, 1985, p. 5.
8. Cited by Martin Honecker, "Capital Punishment in German Protestant Theology," *The Death Penalty and Torture*, 55–56.
9. "The Argument Against the Death Penalty," *The Death Penalty in America*, ed. Hugo Bedau (Garden City, N.Y.: Doubleday, 1964), 167–68.
10. *Encyclopedia Britannica*, ed. Warren E. Preece, vol. 15, s.v. "Punishment," (Chicago: Encyclopedia Britannica Pub. Co., 1978), 283.

11. Charles C. Ryrie, "The Doctrine of Capital Punishment," *Bibliotheca Sacra* 129 (July-September 1972): 211.

12. *New Catholic Encyclopedia*, vol. 3, s.v. "Capital Punishment," (New York: McGraw-Hill, 1967), 79.

13. *Encyclopedia Britannica*, vol. 5, s.v. "Criminal Law," 275.

14. For an analysis of contemporary theonomy, see H. Wayne House and Thomas Ice, *Dominion Theology: Blessing or Curse?* (Portland,Ore.: Multnomah Press, 1988) 27–43, 103–89.

2

Crime and Punishment

Before embarking on the discussion as to whether capital punishment satisfies biblical, moral, sociological, and legal requirements, we need first to examine some basic issues behind punishment in general. These issues include identifying the real, as opposed to the legal, victims of crime, reviewing the history of penal theory, and stating the true reason for punishment.

The Nature of Crime and Punishment

Who Is the Victim of Crime?—Lawyers from ancient Babylon, Greece, Rome, and even Jerusalem would immediately recognize many aspects of a modern American criminal court case. They would, however, be confused by one major difference. Their legal codes considered crime a violation against the victim. These codes emphasized the need for offenders and their families to settle with victims and their families. The offense was considered principally a violation against the victim and the victim's family.[1] Consequently such legal codes provided for retribution to the criminal according to the severity of the crime and restitution to the victim according to the extent of his or her loss. The state, in that day, provided the means of redress but did not act as an offended party.

The Old Testament, for example, required that the offender pay for the victim's loss, often with double or triple damages.

In all cases of illegal possession of an ox, a donkey, a sheep, a garment, or any other lost property about which somebody says, "This is mine," both parties are to bring their cases before the judges. The one whom the judges declare guilty must pay back double to his neighbor. (Exod. 22:9 NASB)

The Code of Hammurabi, a Babylonian legal code that predates the Mosaic Law, also required restitution to the victim:

If a shepherd, to whom oxen or sheep have been given to pasture, have been dishonest or have altered their price, or sold them, they shall call him to account, and he shall restore to their owner oxen and sheep tenfold what he has stolen.[2]

Roman law also required that the victim be compensated:

According to the Law of the Twelve Tables (449 B.C.), convicted thieves had to pay double the value of the stolen goods. If the property was discovered hidden in the thief's house, he had to pay three times its value. If he had resisted the house search, or if he had stolen the object using force, he had to pay four times its value.[3]

By contrast, today's victim is a bystander and the state is treated as the offended party, even receiving restitution in the form of fines. How did this change come about?

American criminal laws are built upon a foundation of English law which, in turn, is built upon a deep foundation of history. Around the time of Christ, England was home to a variety of tribal groups. In about A.D. 600 Ethelbert, ruler of Kent, unified many of these groups under his leadership. As king, he issued a detailed legal code, known as the Laws of Ethelbert, which contained an elaborate system of compensation for victims from criminals. Crime was considered an affront to the victim as an individual, and the offenders and their families were held accountable to the victims and their families.[4]

The Norman Conquest changed all this. When William the Conqueror became king of England he claimed title to all the land, and the people became his vassals. Crime, for William and his followers, was not an attack on the individual victim, but on the ultimate person, the king, and his peace. William's son, Henry I, issued the *Leges Henrici* in 1116. These laws established thirty judicial districts throughout the country and gave the jurisdiction over "certain offenses against the king's peace: arson, robbery, murder, false coinage, and crimes of violence."[5] Criminal punishments were no longer viewed primarily as ways of recompensing victims, but of redressing the injury done to the king. The victim's loss was secondary to that of the king.

The more serious crimes, especially those in which a member of the nobility was the criminal, were considered breaches of faith between the vassal and his lord. The Norman term for such a breach of faith was "felony," and the punishment was the reversion of the criminal's possessions to his lord, usually considered to be the king. As a result of these changes, the victim had no recourse for restitution and had to seek redress through civil action.

English law continued to develop along these lines and has greatly influenced American criminal law. Today civil courts hear cases labeled, e.g., "Smith versus Jones," but criminal court cases are "The State versus Smith." The aggrieved party is the state, while the victims have no remedy for their losses except civil courts.[6] If, then, the courts no longer order restitution as part of a criminal's punishment, why do they inflict punishment at all? Why does the state punish criminals?

Theories of Punishment and Purposes of Punishment

What is the balance among the interests of the criminal, the victim, and the state? What should be the goal of criminal law? For many years philosophers, lawyers, moralists, and theologians have debated the proper objectives of a system of justice and punishment in society. Indeed, our current system of criminal law and punishment is a hybrid of conflicting theories and practices.

Criminal punishment has not always been in the hands of the state. In the thirteenth century Thomas Aquinas argued that the order of society was the result of a divine plan and thus its control was in the hands of the church and her officers. The seventeenth century English philosopher Thomas Hobbes argued that man had surrendered his rights of self-help to the state for protection against transgressors and the chaos

15

of the state of nature. Both theories justified the existence of a temporal state to establish and enforce criminal laws and penalties. But it was not until the late eighteenth century that people began trying to formulate a comprehensive penal philosophy and legal reform. Men such as Sir Samuel Romily, John Howard, and Jeremy Bentham sought to ease legal penalties and restrain capricious judges. In his work, *An Introduction to the Principles of Morals and Legislation* (1789), Bentham argued that men act rationally, seeking pleasure and avoiding pain. Punishment, therefore, should fit the crime without being excessive.[7] In an age where ten-year-old boys were hanged for stealing shoes, reform of the legal process and humanization of penal institutions were long overdue.

By the second half of the nineteenth century criminologists, under the influence of positivism, looked at punishment from a sociological viewpoint. In positivist terms, moral responsibility is of no account, only social responsibility.[8] Hence punishment should consist only of those measures that, taking into account the dangerousness of the offender, needed to be taken to protect society. This approach avoided any aspect of retribution and rehabilitation.

Late in the nineteenth century the most recently formulated theory of punishment, rehabilitation, was put forward. The goal of punishment was not recompense for the victim, retribution to the criminal, protection of society, or the general deterrence of crime. Rather, it was the reformation of the individual criminal. This concept was popular in the first half of this century, but beginning in the 1970s rehabilitation has been criticized and no longer enjoys unrivaled popularity among criminologists.[9]

The history of penal theory has been one of changing concepts of justification for punishment. Each of these has held sway for a time and still continues to influence Western legal thinking. None of these concepts—retribution, deterrence, protection of society, and rehabilitation—has been universally accepted as the final answer to the question, why punish? But we must answer this question if we are to reach a decision on capital punishment. Moreover, we as Christians must find the answer, not in the writings of philosophers and criminologists, but in Scripture. If God has given a clear statement of the reason for punishment, and we believe that he has, then that answer is final. We therefore proceed to consider each of these theories in some detail to determine which one best fits the pattern God has established.

Deterrence—Punishment based on the concept of deterrence is designed to keep others from following the example of the punished offender. This, of course, assumes that people are rational and that they will objectively calculate the risk of suffering the same fate as the convicted criminal. Punishment, according to this view, also serves to reinforce the decision of law-abiding citizens to remain that way. These individuals are not tempted to commit a crime and, when they see crime being punished, their rejection of wrongdoing is reinforced.[10]

Punishment, it may be argued, also deters the criminal from committing other crimes. If a person knows that his or her criminal actions will be punished because he has received punishment for crimes already committed, then that person is less likely to commit a crime. The object of punishment, then, is to teach the offender not to repeat his criminal acts. Since the more serious crimes are the ones that society would most like to deter, then it follows that they are worthy of greater punishment. Thus the individual offender becomes an object lesson to society, and the severity of his punishment depends upon the lesson that the court wishes to teach others. There is no necessary connection between the crime and the punishment inflicted. Criminal laws and punishments make examples of criminals to keep other people from harming society through criminal acts.

Deterrence, as the main justification for punishment, suffers from fatal conflicts with reason and Scripture. As C. S. Lewis points out, there is no requirement under this theory that the one punished be guilty of the crime. If the state's goal is to warn people against certain acts, it is not absolutely necessary that the person punished should be guilty. As long as society thinks him to be guilty and learns its lesson from his punishment, the state will have achieved its end. Any basis of punishment which can be used, in theory at least, to justify the punishment of innocent people cannot be correct.[11]

Second, punishment for the sake of deterrence does not respect the individuality of the criminal. He or she loses personal rights and becomes nothing more than an example to deter others from committing crimes. The main issue in punishment is not the individual criminal, but society in general. The criminal is being used as a means to someone else's

17

end. Punishment becomes whatever the sociologists think is necessary to achieve the desired effect on society. If the motivation is to deter the individual from committing another crime, then the same problem exists. Punishment depends on the opinion of experts as to what will be required to effect individual deterrence, and this will vary with each situation and individual.

Finally, this concept fails to take into account justice as an individually applied concept. In the Old Testament theocracy, for example, an individual was punished because he or she had broken a law and thus earned a specific penalty. Deterrence of future crimes, while a definite aspect of the theocratic penal code (executions by stoning were public), was not the chief object of punishment. The New Testament presents the same concept. A church leader, or elder, may earn increased support by good works or he may earn discipline by breaking God's rules. In both cases the rewards of his conduct are given publicly to reinforce good conduct and to warn others against bad. But the Christian leader is given the individual reward of his own conduct:

> The elders who direct the affairs of the church well are worthy of double honor, especially those whose work is preaching and teaching. . . . Do not entertain an accusation against an elder unless it is brought by two or three witnesses. Those who sin are to be rebuked publicly, so that the others may take warning. (1 Tim. 5:17–20)

Thus, deterrence is not the primary object of punishment in Scripture and does not provide the final answer to the question, why punish?

Protection of Society—Some argue that the basis for punishment of criminal acts is not retribution or deterrence, but the protection of society. This may be accomplished by medical treatment, social retraining, or long-term incarceration. Supporters of this concept argue that criminals should be isolated and treated, usually without their consent, in order to eliminate any future problems when they are returned to society. However, this idea raises a serious problem. The imposition of a life imprisonment sentence for a crime as serious as murder seems a reasonable punishment, but what about the punishment meted out to one who will probably commit a serious crime but who has not yet done so? A nonviolent sex offender, for example, may well

18

be a potential killer, but should he be punished for probable future acts? Condemning a man in advance is essentially unjust.

The protection concept is also open to some of the same fatal biblical objections leveled at the deterrence theory. It also fails to respect the personhood of the criminal in that the treatment is applied without the individual's permission. To be cured against one's will, as C. S. Lewis argues, "is to be classified with infants, imbeciles, and domestic animals."[12]

So the most serious criticism leveled against the deterrence and the protection of society concepts is that they do not respect the dignity of the criminal. Perhaps, then, the proper motive for punishment lies, not in society, but in the rehabilitation of the individual.

Rehabilitation—The most recent theory of punishment is that the chief end of criminal law should be the rehabilitation or reformation of the criminal. Many today argue that an offender should be treated and trained to return to society as a law-abiding member of the community. For example, the Model Penal Code proposed by the American Law Institute in 1962 stated that a basic objective of criminal law should be "to promote the correction and rehabilitation of offenders."[13] As previously mentioned, the term *penitentiary* indicates that jails were to be places for criminals to repent of their crimes.

While the idea of rehabilitating criminals and returning them to society seems to be a worthy goal, it is open to serious objections. One problem recognized by criminologists is that such punishment tends to be indeterminate. Prison sentences are not objectively related to the crime committed, but are subjectively linked to the degree of reform exhibited. This, then, requires that someone measure reform, and thus places the criminal's sentence in the hands of psychological "experts," rather than experienced law professionals. Rehabilitation also assumes that criminals have committed crime because of a lack of training or education, but this is not always the case. Many criminals are well-educated and seemingly equipped to function in society.

Criminologists point to three additional problems with this theory. First, there is little objective proof that rehabilitation has taken place in any effective, systematic way. Indeed, the rising crime rate seems to argue that little or no reformation is being accomplished by the current penal system. A second professional objection to rehabilitation as a basis for punishment is that too much authority is granted to administrators in passing sentence on the offender. There have been cases where those guilty of minor infractions have been subject to long sentences simply because they were unable to or refused to adopt a subservient attitude to those in authority.

Further, the idea of rehabilitation or treatment implies that crime is considered a disease that can be cured, not an act that should be punished. If crime is a mental state, rather than an act, then any state of mind which society does not want, such as religion, can be defined as criminal and subjected to treatment. This is in stark contradiction of the biblical concept that crime is an act to be punished, not a state of mind to be treated. A theory of punishment that would justify the "curing" of any state of mind a given society did not wish to tolerate is a "finer instrument of tyranny than wickedness ever had before."

> It would be vain to plead that states of mind which displease government need not always involve moral turpitude and do not therefore always deserve forfeiture of liberty. For our masters will not be using the concepts of Desert and Punishment but those of disease and cure.[14]

The major biblical arguments against reformation have already been stated as objections against the other views and may be summarized here. There is no direct, necessary connection between the severity of the crime and the resulting punishment. The criminal is treated as an object to be reshaped, rather than a person worthy to receive the just due of his or her deliberate actions. The Bible, in both Old and New Testaments, speaks of appropriate penalties for crimes (Heb. 2:2) with personal reformation of the offender as a secondary, unessential result. The reformation concept, then, does not provide the final answer to the question of why punish. This brings our discussion to the final concept, that of retribution.

Retribution—This is the earliest theory of punishment. The term means to repay and is sometimes used in law, though not commonly in modern times, as the equivalent of "recompense," or a payment or compensation for services, property, use of an estate, or other value received. In this case, the act or service is a criminal offense, and the payment is punishment.

This concept lies behind most ancient laws, including the Code of Hammurabi:

> If a man steal ox or sheep, ass or pig, or boat—if it be from a god (temple) or a palace, he shall restore thirtyfold; if it be from a freeman, he shall render tenfold. If the thief have nothing wherewith to pay he shall be put to death.[15]

Both Old and New Testament references to punishment reflect a retribution foundation:

> If a man steals an ox or a sheep and slaughters it or sells it, he must pay back five head of cattle for the ox and four sheep for the sheep. (Exod. 22:1)

> That servant who knows his master's will and does not get ready or does not do what his master wants will be beaten with many blows. But the one who does not know and does things deserving punishment will be beaten with few blows. (Luke 12:47–48)

This was the prevailing concept of punishment for ancient cultures, and for Western culture up to the eighteenth century.

Retribution treats the criminal as an individual who has committed specific acts and is paying for them. Authorities impose these penalties as an end in themselves, not to achieve any particular social objective (such as rehabilitation of the criminal, deterrence of crime, or protection of society). Supporters of retribution argue that punishment should not be inflicted unless a person has been found guilty of an offense.[16] This excludes collective guilt or transferred punishment such as punishing a whole town for the crime of one resident, or killing a son because a father killed another father's son, as in Babylonian law. Consequently retribution is based on *condignity* (that is, it is well-deserved). Retribution focuses on the criminal as an individual, not as a means to the improvement of society in general. The law treats the offender as one who has earned his punishment by specific criminal acts. Indeed, the concept of desert is the only connecting link between punishment and justice. It is only as deserved or undeserved that a sentence can be just or unjust. Retribution maintains the rights of both human beings, i.e., the criminal as well as the victim.[17]

Retribution also includes the concept of proportionality (not unlimited retaliation), that is, a scale should be used to equate various crimes with various punishments. Usually this is known as the *lex talionis*, that is, "law of retaliation" in which there is "eye-for-eye" penalties. Contrary to popular belief, this is not a license for unlimited retribution, but a necessary limitation on the extent or severity of the punishment. It demands proportionality, not exact equivalence. In other words, a man is punished because he deserves it, but only as much as he deserves.[18] Just retribution or retribution proper necessarily implies the standard of proportionality or equivalency.

> In criminal law this signifies that punishment must be deserved pain, that the criminal gets his due in it. But also with respect to a contractual remuneration or recompense, retribution, in its pregnant sense, implies this requirement that it must be deserved, that it is a determination in a super-arbitrary way of the (juridical) value of the deed upon which it is intended to react.[19]

Others have argued that retribution protects the criminal by setting fixed penalties before the commission of a crime. The punishment would have, at least in theory, consistency of application so that the criminal would know in advance what his debt or punishment is. Restitution also protects the victim by establishing a framework for individual restitution. This protects the victim from loss by the damage inflicted on him. Currently the victim's only recourse is to attempt, at his own expense, to recover damages in civil courts. Under a retributive model, the individual wronged and the society damaged would receive a just recompense for their losses.[20] As Dougall and Emmett argue,

> Punishment is punishment only where it is deserved. We pay the penalty, because we owe it, and for no other reason and if punishment is inflicted for any other reason whatever than because it is merited by wrong, it is a gross immorality, a crying injustice, and abominable crime, and not what it pretends to be. We may have regard for whatever considerations we please—our own convenience, the

good of society, the benefit of the offender. . . . But these are external to the matter, they cannot give us a right to punish, and nothing can do that but criminal desert.[21]

Retribution is also humane because it honors the criminal by treating him as a rational being with a choice of conduct, even though the choice he made is culpable.[22] Further, retribution is the only connecting link between punishment and justice.

Retribution, however, seems to have one major problem from the Christian perspective. It seems to contradict God's love and limit his mercy. How can God establish a penal system in which punishments are both defined and mandatory? This may display his justice, but surely it eliminates any display of his mercy and love. How, then, can God be both merciful and just within the context of a retributive penal system?

Love, mercy, justice, and the other characteristics of God are not component parts of a whole. Each of these describes his total being. Love, for example, is not a part of God's nature; God in his total being is love. While God may display one quality or another at a given time, no quality is independent or preeminent over any of the others. Whenever God displays his wrath, he is still love. When he shows his love, he does not abandon his holiness. This is summarized in Exodus 34:6–7:

And he passed in front of Moses, proclaiming, "The LORD, the Lord, the compassionate and gracious God, slow to anger, abounding in love and faithfulness, maintaining love to thousands, and forgiving wickedness, rebellion and sin. Yet he does not leave the guilty unpunished; he punishes the children and their children for the sin of the fathers to the third and fourth generation.(NIV)

The outworking of justice is based upon the character of God. He is indeed a loving God, but is also a God who is holy, just, and righteous. Such a God demands holiness and righteousness from people and any unrighteousness cannot go unpunished. Therefore, although the Scriptures contain elements of judgment and forgiveness, these actions are not in contradiction, but are complementary parts of God's character and his dealings with people. Hence both Old and New Testaments sanctioned capital punishment. Whether or not we like it, the death penalty is compatible with the nature of God. This, however, does not demand its application, but certainly the concept of retribution supports it, and the biblical data permit it.

While some Christians incorrectly reject retribution as contradictory to the character of God, a number of criminologists find the concept contradictory to their view of modern society. For example, Harvard law professor and criminologist, Sheldon Glueck writes that "No thoughtful person today seriously holds this theory of sublimated social vengeance. . . ."[23] Glueck and others attack retribution by equating it with personal vengeance, a distasteful concept that has no place in our enlightened society. Others reject retribution as too "primitive" to be applied to our modern age. Since the concept of retribution is foundational to the biblical concept of punishment and the death penalty, these objections will be answered in detail in the next section.

Objections to Retribution and Responses to the Objections

1. *Retribution is also a crime.*

Supposedly, in retaliation the punisher is just as guilty as the criminal. This view is a response to an incorrect understanding of the "eye for an eye" statement (Exod. 21:23, Lev. 24:19–20, and Deut. 19:21). It views retribution as "a grim, literal equivalence of crime to punishment where both are equal as to essence and degree, so the punisher has as much moral guilt as the criminal."[24]

Response:

Retribution, apart from the limiting concept of proportionality, can become a crime in itself. But the principle of an eye for an eye places strict limits on retributive punishment. An eye cannot be taken in punishment unless an eye has been taken in a crime. The punishment must fit the crime; it cannot exceed the seriousness of the offense.

Briefly stated . . . , the retribution of biblical law did not require precise reciprocation. Rather, it exhibited the rule of proportionate recompense, a distinctively retributive principle.[25]

2. *Retribution is merely vindictive revenge.*

Oliver Wendell Holmes called retribution "a disguise for vengeance."[26] Many today agree with him. Glueck, for example, claims that

> official social institutions should not be predicated upon the destructive emotion of vengeance, which is not only the expression of an infantile way of solving a problem, but unjust and destructive of the purpose of protecting society.[27]

The criminal becomes the victim and the victim becomes the criminal as the offended releases feelings of anger and hurt on the offender. Vengeance, William White claims, seems to be the original motive for what is now termed justice.[28]

Response:

Revenge and retribution are decidedly different. Properly understood, retribution does not substitute for revenge, but protects the guilty party against the revenge of his or her victims. Revenge is intensely personal, a desire to inflict injury in return for injury. It is born out of outrage, anger, and a deep-seated sense of personal violation. Retribution, on the other hand, is a dispassionate, controlled judicial process in which punishment is meted out by proper authority after a thorough investigation of the facts of the case. Retribution itself is not a feeling, and its origin is not found in the feeling of revenge. It is the dispassionate, just payment (not repayment) of the penalty an individual has earned by his or her criminal acts. As Sparks notes,

> Retribution invariably opposes unbridled revenge. Retribution binds every exercise of will within limits. What is completely just from a retributive standpoint may very well leave revenge unsatisfied.[29]

3. Retribution is primitive.

A number of critics reject retribution because they claim that it is a primitive concept. Glueck, for one, writes that "out of this primitive root [retribution] there has grown the traditional, classical criminal law."[30] Paton describes retribution as an "antiquated doctrine."[31] With retribution we "restrict human freedom and inflict the misery of punishment on human beings, things which seem to belong to the prehistory of morality and to be quite hostile to its general spirit."[32]

These and other critics properly recognize that the concept of retribution has been the foundation of criminal law in many ancient

25

cultures. Modern thinking, they maintain, has evolved beyond these archaic categories and entertains new, more valid concepts. Since retribution has been the basis of many ancient criminal codes, it cannot possibly be applicable to modern society.

Response:

It is, of course, chauvinistic to equate antiquity with worthlessness. The concept of retribution has the endorsement of most of the world's ancient cultures, including that of Old Testament Israel. Rejection of the idea because of its historical longevity betrays an evolutionary bias in the critics' thinking. Rejection of retribution must be based on criteria other than its age.

This position has been recognized by evangelicals and applied to other areas of biblical ethics. For example, few would argue for rejecting the biblical concept of marriage for life because of its ancient heritage. So it is with retribution. In the Old Testament God ordained retribution as the foundation for Israel's criminal justice system and continued the concept in the New Testament. In terms of history, this makes retribution ancient, but in terms of authority this makes it valid.

4. It is not utilitarian.

Most modern criminologists argue that the goal of punishment should serve utilitarian ends such as rehabilitation or deterrence, personal or general. Glueck, for one, states that

> Society's legal institutions are concerned with the utilitarian possibilities of a punishment regime, possibilities which are founded upon the social purpose of the machinery of justice, namely, the maintenance of the general security with as little interference with the individual's rights as a human being and citizen as is necessary for the achievement of that social purpose.[33]

Retribution does not fit into this mold, for it proposes to pay an individual the deserts of his actions without regard to utilitarian motives. Consequently, many modern criminologists reject the concept as a valid basis for punishment.

Response:

Rehabilitation of criminals, the deterrence of crime, and the protection of society from crime are valid and proper concerns of a

26

legal system. However, they cannot be its ultimate goal, for they ignore the criminal's individuality, his rights to personally receive the payment of his acts, and his freedom to be treated as a person in terms of punishment. Retribution offers objective rewards for specific behavior, rewards proportional to the conduct. Do this, the law says, and you will receive that. Rehabilitation, on the other hand, takes punishment out of the objective law code into the subjective realm of psychology. Punishment would depend on the opinion of psychological experts and can vary from person to person. No one can claim that a given punishment is disproportionate, for sentences are placed "in the hands of technical experts whose special sciences do not even employ such categories as rights or justice."[34] A human being has a basic right to the objective rewards of his or her actions, and without a retributive system of penalties the criminal faces an indefinite sentence which would end only when the psychological experts declared the individual rehabilitated. Crime becomes a disease, not moral guilt, and patients are not cured until the doctor pronounces them well.

All this could imply that retributive justice has no concern for the individual or society, that it could show no mercy and compassion. In reality, this is the case of the utilitarian concepts of criminal law. These do not recognize moral guilt and personal responsibility. Consequently, they cannot show either mercy or justice.

> The distinction between mercy and justice is essential. Mercy tempers justice. The essential act of mercy is to pardon and pardon in its very essence involves the recognition of guilt and ill-desert in the recipient. If crime is only a disease which needs cure, not sin which deserves punishment, it cannot be pardoned. Mercy, detached from justice, grows unmerciful.[35]

The Biblical Basis for Retribution

We have considered retribution as a concept of criminal justice and answered the important objections to it. Our next step is to discuss the biblical basis for retribution. The most commonly cited biblical teaching on this subject is "eye for an eye," known as the *lex talionis*, or law of

THE DEATH PENALTY DEBATE

retribution. This statement, part of a larger summation of Israel's revealed legal system, is repeated three times:

> *Exodus 21:23b–25* NASB: "you shall appoint as a penalty life for life, eye for eye, tooth for tooth, hand for hand, foot for foot, burn for burn, wound for wound, bruise for bruise."

> *Leviticus 24:19–20* NASB: "and if a man injures his neighbor, just as he has done, so it shall be done to him: fracture for fracture, eye for eye, tooth for tooth; just as he has injured a man, so it shall be inflicted on him."

> *Deuteronomy 19:21* NASB in reference to false witnesses: "Thus you shall not show pity: life for life, eye for eye, tooth for tooth, hand for hand, foot for foot."

This summarizes the retributive nature of Yahweh's theocratic criminal justice system. The punishment will fit the crime and the severity of the punishment cannot exceed the severity of the crime. God thus placed strict limits on the retributive punishment to be meted out to criminals.

Black's Law Dictionary, for example, refers the researcher of *retaliation* to *lex talionis*, defined as

> the law of retaliation which requires the infliction upon a wrong-doer of the same injury which he has caused to another. Expressed in the Mosaic Law by the formula, "an eye for an eye, a tooth for a tooth," etc. In modern international law, the term describes the rule by which one state may inflict upon the citizens of another state death, imprisonment, or other hardship, in retaliation for similar injuries imposed upon its own citizens.[36]

Not all, however, have understood this concept. A cursory reading of these biblical verses above could easily lead to viewing retribution as nothing more than simple vindictiveness or "getting back at someone." But the very context of these passages, especially the Exodus reference, argues against such an interpretation. In the case where no serious injury was incurred a monetary fine could be imposed, but more severe injury demanded a more severe punishment. The broader context of Exodus 20–23 shows that biblical law is not based on personal retaliation or revenge, but on proportionate compensation:

> The law of damages is that one who injures or wrongs another shall make restitution. Rules concerning the duty of restitution, and the amount or measurement of damages are stated in the Scriptures. Thus restitution is required of a thief (Exodus 22:3), of one who causes a field or vineyard to be "eaten" (Exodus 22:5), of one who kindles a fire which escapes and burns "stacks of corn, or the standing corn, or the field" of another (Exodus 22:10, 12), and of one who kills an animal belonging to another.[37]

The New Testament also assumes the Old Testament concept of retribution. Hebrews 2:2 assures us that "every transgression and disobedience received a just recompense." The writer is not developing a full-orbed commentary on the Mosaic Law at this point, but is establishing the foundation of his subsequent argument. His discussion of the sacrifice of Christ will make no sense unless his readers agree on the concept of retribution as established by the Mosaic Law. The writer assumes the validity of retribution, informs his readers of this assumption, and begins building his argument.

More to the point, however, is Paul's development of justification by faith in Romans 3. First, he established mankind's guilt beyond any reasonable doubt. "All have sinned!" he declares. This guilt merits a just retribution. Since the offence is against the holy God, the proportionate punishment is death. The retribution was made, though it fell on a divinely provided substitute—Jesus. He suffered the exact proportionate punishment man deserved. Forgiveness is not free, but rather it is satisfied retribution. It is by Christ's death that God is both just and justifier.[38] Thus the Old and New Testaments recognize retribution as basic to God's theocratic government and the salvation he offers to all people.

An Overview of the Biblical Case for Capital Punishment

One may grant the biblical basis of retribution but still reject the concept of capital punishment. This, then, is our next question: What does the Scripture teach about the death penalty? This concept includes the ideas that (1) a crime has been committed, (2) the person executed is actually guilty, and (3) that the government which carries out the sentence has been duly constituted.[39]

The first reference to capital punishment is Genesis 9:6—"Whoever sheds the blood of man, by man shall his blood be shed for in the image of God has God made man." Murder, the shedding of man's blood by man, is declared to be a capital crime because of the unique value of human life. Mankind bears the *imago Dei,* and the willful termination of an embodiment of that image merits the ultimate penalty—death. This principle extends to the entire human race because Noah, to whom it was given, stood at the head of a new beginning of the human race. Principles given to Noah were not confined to any group, family, or cult.[40]

The death penalty was part of the Mosaic code. A number of offenses were designated as capital crimes, including murder (Exod. 21:12; Num. 35:16–31), working on the Sabbath (Exod. 35:2), cursing father or mother (Lev. 20:9), adultery (Lev. 20:10), incest (Lev. 20:11–13), sodomy (Lev. 20:15–16), false prophesying (Deut. 13:1–10;18:20), idolatry (Deut. 17:2–7), incorrigible juvenile delinquency (Deut. 21:18–23), rape (Deut. 22:25), keeping an ox known to be dangerous if the ox had killed a human being (Exod. 21:29), kidnapping (Exod. 21:16), and intrusion of an alien into a sacred place or office (Num. 1:51; 3:10, 38; 18:7).

In the Gospels, Jesus recognized the Mosaic Law, including the death penalty. In the pericope of John 8:1–11 he did not abrogate the Mosaic command to stone adulteresses. He challenged the motivation of the accusers, rather than the validity of the capital punishment.

Another unmistakable New Testament reference to capital punishment is Romans 13:1–7. Human government is ordained by God as a distinct sphere of authority, separate from the home and the church. Government is to be obeyed as the only social authority established by God for the opposition of evil in the world (as opposed to the church). In the exercise of this authority government has the right to taxation and the right to enforce its rules. Paul's phrase, "the right to bear sword," extends to the right of capital punishment.[41] Only government, not the church (in discipline), or the family (in vengeance), can practice capital punishment. God, through the apostle Paul, authorizes duly established governments to exercise certain rights over all of their citizens, specifically including taxation and capital punishment. Hence the death penalty is permitted by the New Testament.

Capital punishment does not contradict God's prohibition against murder. Indeed, the theocratic government of Old Testament Israel set the death penalty as the retributive penalty for murder. The Decalogue proscribed murder, not all killing. If the sixth commandment be extended to outlaw all taking of human life, then God himself became a transgressor of the Law by establishing capital punishment and ordering its application on several occasions.[42] There is a distinction between killing and murdering, a distinction that is recognized in both Old and New Testaments.[43]

The biblical purpose of capital punishment is the promotion of retributive justice by civil government. It is the purpose of government to punish those who do evil (2 Peter 2:13), and capital punishment is evidently one of the ways this purpose is to be promoted.[44] The New Testament gives few detailed instructions on the functioning of civil government. Therefore it is up to the government and its citizens to establish how specific administrative details are to be carried out. The New Testament gives no hint that murder does not require the death penalty in the new dispensation, and it is silent about other capital crimes. The point of this discussion, however, is to establish the fact that the Bible makes capital punishment a valid retribution which does not contradict God's character or his revelation. This we have done.

What About Exceptions?

What about the biblical exceptions? Do they invalidate the norm that life is to be taken for life? We do not think so.

Retributive Justice in the David and Bathsheba Incident

The question is often raised as to why David did not die for his sins of adultery and murder (2 Sam. 11:1–12:23). The fact that David did not suffer the death penalty seems on the surface to contradict the theory of retributive justice. But closer inspection shows that justice and mercy were both served. David's act of murder brought murder into his house

31

(2 Sam. 12:10–11), and his adultery resulted in the public violation of his wives (2 Sam. 12:11–12). Further, the child conceived in this adultery died. But David himself was spared. Where then is the retribution in his case?

When Nathan reproved him, David acknowledged his own ill-desert and accepted the judgment he had pronounced against Nathan's hypothetical villain, which was consistent with the recompense outlined in Exodus 21:37. Then he appealed to Yahweh, not on the basis of justice, but on the basis of his mercy, grace, and covenantal love. David pleaded for mercy because he knew that he was justly condemned before Yahweh. Indeed, David's plea for mercy assumes the reality of the death penalty. Yahweh's forgiveness was publicly extended to David by Nathan and probably also by a priest, thereby removing the governmental requirement from the nation so Israel did not have to carry out the death sentence.

When David appealed to God's sovereign favor, steadfast loyalty, and yearning love, God's retributive justice was not being denied. Rather, it was this motivation that drove David to seek his help. He was forced to seek Yahweh's unmerited favor by the threat of his own certain, merited disfavor. "The *just recompense expected* drove David to seek His mercy. God's mercy forgave David; the Cross ultimately satisfied God's justice."[45]

NOTES

1. Daniel W. Van Ness, *Crime and Its Victims*, 64; see bibliography.
2. "Code of Hammurabi," trans. Robert Francis Harper (Chicago: University of Chicago Press, 1904), sec. 265.
3. Van Ness, *Crime and Its Victims*, 65.
4. Ibid., 68.
5. Ibid., 66.
6. Ibid., 68.
7. Jeremy Bentham, *An Introduction to the Principles of Morals and Legislation*, 1789 cited in *Encyclopedia Britannica*, vol. 15, 15th ed. (Chicago: Helen Hemingway Benton, Publisher, 1975), 283.
8. *New Catholic Encyclopedia*, vol 7, "Humanitarianism," (New York: McGraw-Hill, 1967), 229.
9. *Encyclopedia Britannica*, "Punishment," 284.
10. Ibid., "Deterence," 283.
11. C. S. Lewis, *God in the Dock: Essays on Theology and Ethics*, 291–92.
12. Ibid., 292.
13. *Encyclopedia Britannica*, "Criminal Law," 275.

14. Lewis, *God in the Dock*, 293.
15. "Code of Hammurabi," sec. 8.
16. *Encyclopedia Britannica*, "Punishment," 807.
17. Lewis, *God in the Dock*, 288.
18. Ibid., 287.
19. Hermann Dooyeweerd, *A New Critique of Theoretical Thought, Volume II* (Philadelphia: Presbyterian and Reformed, 1969), 130.
20. Larry S. Fletcher, "Retributive Justice in the David and Bathsheba Incident," unpublished Th.M thesis, Dallas Theological Seminary, 1980.
21. Lily Dougall and Cyril Emmet, *The Lord of Thought* (London: Student Christian Movement, 1922).
22. Fletcher, "Retributive Justice," 2.
23. Sheldon Glueck, *Crime and Correction*, "Principles of a Rational Penal Code," 75; see bibliography.
24. Fletcher, "Retributive Justice," 4.
25. Ibid., 5.
26. Oliver Wendell Holmes, Jr., *The Common Law* (Boston: Little, Brown, 1881), 45.
27. Glueck, *Crime and Correction*, 30.
28. William A. White, *Insanity and Criminal Law* (New York: Macmillan, 1923), 13–15.
29. John A. Sparks, "The Reconstruction of the Criminal Law: Retribution Revisited," *Journal of Christian Reconstruction* 3 (Winter, 1976–1977): 135–37.
30. Glueck, *Crime and Correction*, 56.
31. George W. Paton, *A Textbook of Jurisprudence*, 4th ed. (Oxford: Clarendon Press, 1972), 359.
32. Herbert Lionel Adolphus Hart, *Law, Liberty and Morality* (London: Oxford University Press, 1961), 83.
33. Glueck, *Crime and Correction*, 76.
34. Lewis, *God in the Dock*, 288–89.
35. Ibid., 293–94.
36. "Lex talionis," *Black's Law Dictionary*, 5th ed. (St. Paul: West Publishing, 1979), 822.
37. Harold Ballard Clark, *Biblical Law*, 2nd ed. (Portland, Ore.: Binfords and Mort, 1944), 296–97.
38. Fletcher, "Retributive Justice," 11–12; and Ernest Findley Scott, *Paul's Epistle to the Romans* (London: SCM Press, 1947).
39. Charles C. Ryrie, "The Doctrine of Capital Punishment," *Bibliotheca Sacra* 129 (July-September 1972): 211.
40. Ibid., 213.
41. Ibid., 214–16.
42. There were times when God did not exact the death penalty when the situation seemed to require it, such as when Cain killed Abel.
43. Ryrie, "Capital Punishment," 216.
44. Ibid., 217.
45. Fletcher, "Retributive Justice," 53.

3

Capital Punishment in the Old Testament

There is no doubt that Yahweh encouraged, commanded, and personally enforced the death penalty during the Old Testament era. When he established his covenant with Noah following the Deluge he made capital punishment an integral part of the covenantal formula (Gen. 9:5–6).[1] Yahweh clearly included the death penalty in the Mosaic Law (cf. Exod. 21:12–17), ordered the stoning of a Sabbath-breaker, and rewarded Phinehas for executing a sinning Israelite (Num. 25:6–13). However, Calvary stands between us and Sinai. We must ask, therefore, if the Old Testament support of capital punishment is in effect after the sacrifice of Jesus. The answer lies in the proper interpretation and application of two foundational relationships: the Noachian Covenant and the Mosaic Covenant.

The Covenant With Noah—The first direct reference to capital punishment is found in Genesis 9:5–6:

And for your lifeblood I will surely demand an accounting. I will demand an accounting from every animal. And from each man, too, I will demand an accounting for the life of his fellow man.

> Whosoever sheds the blood of man,
> by man shall his blood be shed;
> for in the image of God
> has God made man. (NIV)

35

This passage is foundational to the debate among believers concerning the validity of capital punishment in today's society.[2] Therefore, it is important to analyze this passage in its literary and historical contexts to discover whether it does in fact support the death penalty as a proper exercise of governmental authority today. When all the biblical data are evaluated, we will argue that Genesis 9:6 not only permitted capital punishment for murder in Noah's day, but supports the death penalty for murder today as well.

The Context of Genesis 9:6

The author of Genesis separated the major literary divisions of the book with the phrase "this is the account of." The first division (Gen. 1:1–2:4) discusses the heavens and the earth, the second (Gen. 2:5–5:1) describes the experiences of Adam, and the third (Gen. 5:2–6:9) centers on Noah and the events leading to the Flood. Chapter 9 ends this third section by completing the account of the Noachian Deluge. This pericope begins in 8:20 when Noah builds an altar following his exit from the ark. There he offered the proper sacrifices, and God responded by establishing a covenant "with Noah and his sons" (9:1).

This covenant contained three major sections. In the first (Gen. 9:1–3), God commanded Noah's family to increase in number, placed the fear of mankind in all animals, and gave Noah and his sons authority to eat animals as well as plants. In the second section, (Gen. 9:4–6), God placed significant limits on this authority to take animal life. The life-principles of the animal world had come from God and consequently were to be respected. Therefore, he commanded people not to eat meat which contained blood which is representative of life. Then he placed an even stronger prohibition on taking human life. God himself would demand an accounting for the murder of a human being, whether at the hand of man or the paw of an animal. In the third section of the covenant (Gen. 9:8–11), God promised that no flood would ever destroy the earth as had just happened. Noah and his family—the entire human race—thus began life in a new world with new rules, responsibilities, and restrictions. Genesis 9:6 is an integral part of this new order.

A proper understanding of the historical setting of this passage is basic to a correct interpretation of its contents. The most significant event since creation had just ended. Noah, his extended family, and the animals with him in the ark have just left the safety of that ship and stepped into a world physically and spiritually sterile. A flood of global proportions had exterminated all previous animal and human life.

Like Adam before him, Noah looked out on a world of new beginnings with seemingly unlimited potential. Unlike Adam, however, Noah remembered a previous world inhabited by animals and, above all, people like himself. These individuals had traced their lineage to Adam and their value to the image of the Creator-God resident within them. Noah remembered all this, but it was just a memory, for all previous inhabitants of his former world had been killed by their Creator in one cataclysmic act of universal judgment. When Noah built the altar and prepared the sacrifices, he may well have wondered about the nature of the Creator and the value he placed on life. Had the Creator changed into the Destroyer? Had God's value system shifted so that life—animal and human—had less value in his sight? Possibly Noah wondered this, even as he worshiped.

In this context God spoke, and established the first recorded covenant between himself and mankind. Surely a covenant (something that was in all probability familiar to Noah) was called for in light of what had transpired. So God entered into a formal contract with mankind (Noah and his family) to assure them that the judgment was past, his holiness was satisfied, and his concern for life continued. Above all, God reassured mankind that, as the bearers of his image, they still possessed unique value and their lives were of supreme importance to him.

> The passage is completely given over to God's initiative in making a covenant with all humankind. The repetition of the commission given to Adam demonstrates that with Noah there is a new beginning, but one that required a covenant. It was now necessary to have promises from God because people might begin to wonder whether God held life cheap or whether the taking of life was a small matter. This covenant through Noah declared that God held life sacred and that humankind too must preserve life in the earth.[3]

Noah was given the same commission as Adam, "fill the earth," but there was more. The significant point of Genesis 9:1–17 is that God instituted a new civil order for mankind which would be the basis of his dealings, not just with Israel, but with all of mankind. Under this new order animals may be killed for food, but even animal life, represented by the blood, must be respected because of its ultimate source. The life-principle must be symbolically returned to that source, not consumed as a mundane piece of meat. Human life, already differentiated from that of animals by the presence of God's image, is given additional value and protection. Life is God's, especially human life, and he alone will determine its end. The deliberate taking of human life, whether by man or animal, will bring retributive judgment from God, not personal vengeance from men. As Lloyd Bailey says,

> Life originated by a special act of the Deity (by the power of the divine breath, as the ancient story in Genesis 2:7 put it). Consequently, humans were not free to terminate it, save under conditions specified by God. Even food animals must be brought to the sanctuary and slaughtered in a prescribed ritual whereby the blood is removed. Failure to do so results in "bloodguilt" (Leviticus 17:4), a term which is elsewhere used for the murder of a human being (Exodus 22:2). How much more the offense, therefore, if human life ("created in the image of God," Genesis 1:26) is taken without proper sanction! One has acted arrogantly against a life-force that is an extension of God's own life-giving power. It is, to put it baldly, "an attack upon God." Even an animal that kills a human is to be destroyed (Exodus 21:28). A human who does so all the more forfeits any right to life (Genesis 9:1–7).[4]

There can be no question that God is establishing a new order at the outset of a new period of human history. But were the provisions of that new order given as universal concepts applicable to all men from Noah to the present, or were they limited to a specific group and/or time and thus have no application today? The question is foundational to the issue of capital punishment, for if this covenant established the authority of government to apply the death penalty, and if that authority is established on a universal basis, then these passages teach that capital punishment is permissible today. If, however, its application is limited so that it does not apply to the present time, then the Noachian

Covenant cannot be used to support the validity of capital punishment today.

The Scope of Genesis 9:6

Several key observations support the idea that the Noachian Covenant covers all of humanity and is in effect today. Baker, for example, argues for the universal and ongoing nature of the mandate from its context:

> There are several factors in the context which make it clear that the Noahic Covenant and the mandate for capital punishment contained in it are enduring: (1) seasons (Gen. 8:22) were instituted which continue as a part of the natural order (2) the dread of man by animals continues as a basic relationship between man and the animal kingdom (Gen. 9:2); (3) the eating of meat is still permitted (Gen. 9:3); (4) no flood has again destroyed the earth (Gen. 9:11), of which the rainbow serves as a continuing pledge (Gen. 9:16–17); and (5) the violation of the image of God continues to be a reason for exacting the extreme penalty (Gen. 9:6).[5]

Several other important factors are worthy of note. First, the command to carry out the death penalty in Genesis 9:6 is made before the institution of the Mosaic Law. Second, the Mosaic Law did not abrogate any of the stipulations of the Noachian Covenant. The conditions of the Mosaic Covenant, and the death penalty in particular, were given to Israel whereas the Noachian Covenant was universal in scope and application. Third, Noah was not a Hebrew. As a generic human being, he serves as the representative head of a new order of mankind, not just Jews, but of mankind in general. As Noah and his extended family stood before the Lord they were the only human beings on earth. They were the totality of mankind. Consequently, the table of nations in Genesis is traced to Noah as the source of a new earthly lineage.

Another factor that needs to be taken into consideration is that specific pre-Mosaic covenants are still in effect. The apostle Paul argued that the Abrahamic Covenant was still in effect (and presumably still is) when he wrote

What I mean is this: The law, introduced 430 years later, does not set aside the covenant previously established by God and thus do away with the promise. (Gal. 3:17)

Baker stresses the importance of this fact:

No effort is being made to identify Genesis 9:6 with the Abrahamic covenant, and it is fully recognized by the author that the covenant to Abraham is in effect despite the institution of the Law of Moses, not its abolition. But the fact remains that something which preceded the Law is still in effect, according to Paul, simply because of its intrinsic nature and priority. Does that not allow for the possibility that Genesis 9:6 might still remain in force?[6]

We argue that Paul's statement does establish the possibility that the Noachian Covenant continues today, and we further argue that this covenant is in fact still in force as the foundational relationship between God and mankind in general. So Baker writes:

The important thing to observe is that Noah and his family stood at the beginning of a new human civilization to which new powers and dominion were given for the first time. The civilization branched out into all the races and nationalities which are known today. Only one of these was Israel, to whom the Law was given. The covenant with Noah was with him and his posterity. Much of that posterity lived and died never having heard the Law of Moses but carried into its laws and traditions the basic elements of the covenant with Noah, including the right of man to punish man with death for the crime of murder. It is rather ironic that Israel . . . may have been among those who least observed this law, even though they possessed the clearest mandate of it in the Old Testament Scriptures.[7]

Views on the Universality of the Noachian Covenant

Not everyone, however, agrees that the Noachian Covenant is universal, for some argue that it was limited. Three general arguments are offered along these lines.

The Expiation View. The expiatory viewpoint of Genesis 9:6 draws a necessary connection between the expiation or removal of sin that the Levitical sacrifices accomplished and the death of a murderer.[8] This view follows through with the Old Testament imagery of people offering the required sacrifices for the expiation of their sins. These sacrifices served as types of the ultimate sacrifice, Jesus Christ, whose death on the cross removes sin once for all (cf. 1 John 2:2). The death penalty prescribed in Genesis 9:6 is said to be speaking largely to the issue of expiation. The argument follows that, since expiatory sacrifices were done away with by the death of Christ, so, too, is the death penalty.[9]

This view, however, is open to several fatal objections. First, although the connection between expiation and capital punishment is noticed in subsequent Levitical legislation (e.g., Numbers 35:31–33), expiation is not readily apparent or even implied in Genesis 9:6. Second, this view overlooks certain key features of Genesis 9:6 such as the universality of the context and the unambiguous language of retribution. This is especially significant when considering the phrase "image of God" and its importance for the universality of the Genesis mandate. Third, there is a failure to differentiate between expiatory sacrifice and expiatory punishment. Baker discusses this in some detail:

Punishment is necessarily connected with wrongdoing and guilt. It can only be justified as the expiation or satisfaction for guilt. In other words, when a crime is committed under civil law, an expiation to the law or society is necessarily made in the form of a prescribed punishment. The law is "satisfied" when the offender suffers his punishment (expiates for his crime). However, when an expiatory sacrifice is made in the Old Testament, the victim is not "punished" in any way for sins it [the animal sacrifice] has committed rather, the victim takes the punishment due to the one offering it. This is substitutionary and therefore is typical of Christ's sacrifice. Capital punishment was in no way typical of the sacrifice of Christ, even though Christ suffered his death under a law demanding capital punishment, for it involved the punishment of one who was guilty of his crime. Christ assumed as substitute the guilt of the human race, but he could do this only because he was sinless or guiltless. For capital punishment to have to have been fulfilled in the sacrifice of Christ, therefore, it would have to have been typical.[10]

In brief, the expiatory view confuses the significance of sacrifice and punishment, and does not provide full consideration of the universal-contextual implications of Genesis 9:1–7.

The Descriptive View. A second view is that Genesis 9:6 is not prescriptive in nature, but rather descriptive or predictive.[11] That is, the text describes what will happen to the murderer, either at the hands of men, or, ultimately, at the hand of God. As noted in the previous chapter, Malcom A. Reid argues that

> Verse 5 simply states that God will demand an accounting from those who kill other people and that verse 6 is God's realistic recognition that fallen men will seek blood vengeance.[12]

Reid first of all rejects verses 5 and 6 as central to the entire passage because they do not distinguish between murder and killing. Indeed, if capital punishment is actually in view, then, according to verse 5, animals may be guilty of murder and liable for trial, sentencing, and execution. Since this conclusion is unreasonable, Reid argues that the passage describes a general response on God's part to killing. However, he fails to recognize that verse 5 states a general principle from which the law of verse 6 is drawn. Verse 6 is a form of apodictic law while verse 5 is simply the principle from which the law is drawn.[13]

Reid's second argument is that the Hebrew verb *yissapek*, "shall be shed," should be translated predictively rather than prescriptively. Proponents of capital punishment favor the prescriptive translation and point to the phrase "by man" to justify this approach. Reid, however, argues that they are guilty of defective reasoning by appealing to the prepositional phrase to establish their interpretation of the verb, rather than considering the verb's tense apart from the phrase. Unfortunately for Reid's case, the nature of the Hebrew imperfect tense allows it to be translated either as a predictive or a prescriptive action. The context is the deciding factor, and the presence of the prepositional phrase, "by man," is clear support for the prescriptive translation.

Capital Punishment in the Old Testament

Reid's last argument is based on the general nature of verse 5. Every killing, he argues, would mandate capital punishment, so it seems that no killing would be allowed. In making this generalization he overlooks the distinction between murder and prescribed killing. The same God who authored the sixth commandment, "You shall not commit murder," (Exod. 20:13), also commanded the armies of Israel to obliterate the Canaanite tribes who lived in the land promised to Abraham (e.g., Josh. 6:15–21). Personal, premeditated murder is forbidden, but governmental acts of killing can be, and have been, prescribed by God. If all killing is murder, then either the text or God lacks integrity. Reid's argument is invalid.

There are other reasons for rejecting the descriptive view. One could concede its plausibility if Genesis 9:6 was considered in isolation. However, the context of Genesis 9:1–7 militates against such a notion. The pericope of 9:1–7 is introduced with imperative verbs, and prohibitions are interspersed throughout which strongly indicate that Yahweh "is directing not laconically describing reality."[14] Verse 5 alone contains three "I will demand" statements. Moreover, the descriptive view does not grapple with the personal element of the language of Genesis 9:6: "And surely your blood of your lives will I require." Finally, the descriptive view assumes, ipso facto, that man will ultimately face judgment within his lifetime for his crime apart from the intervention of human government. Notwithstanding, it is crucial to note that Genesis 9:6, does in fact, provide a foundation for civil government. Baker admirably clarifies this point:

This [the foundation for civil government] is substantiated by the phrase, "Image of God," which limits the infliction of punishment so that it was not left to the whim of individuals but belonged to those who sought for justice and who therefore represent the authority and majesty of God.[15]

In a word, the descriptive view of Genesis 9:6 does not do justice to the textual data and cannot be sustained.

The Historic-Localized View. A third opposing viewpoint is that Genesis 9:6 refers to personal and/or clan vengeance rather than prescribed civil retribution.[16] The key to understanding this argument is the phrase "every man's brother" (9:5). The term "brother," the argument goes, should be limited strictly to a tribal or close of kin context. If the passage is historically conditioned by a localized familial set of circumstances, it follows that the prohibition of Genesis 9:6 is limited in its scope to the tribal milieu of the Noachian age.[17]

The historic-localized view is found wanting on the basis of the following considerations. First, to limit the phrase "every man's brother" (Gen. 9:5) strictly to personal or clan vengeance overlooks the uniqueness of the circumstances of Genesis 9:6 as well as standard usage of the term "brother." Steven James discusses the problem of limiting "every man's brother" to a localized familial life-setting:

> . . . in the context of Genesis 9:5–6 all of humanity comprised only eight persons who were related by blood or marriage. If one of them committed a crime, of necessity he or she would have been punished at the hand of a relative. This situation would have remained true for several generations during which "every man's brother" constituted every member of society. Along this same line of reasoning, the Semitic use of kinship terms extends beyond actual family relationships to include large groups of persons (for examples, cf. Deut. 15:2; 19:15–21; Lev. 25). The term "brother" used in Genesis 9:5 may legitimately be interpreted as meaning all of society, whether literally as was the case for the few generations after Noah, or figuratively as indicated by later biblical use of the term.[18]

Second, even if the context of Genesis 9:6 were limited to personal and tribal vengeance, those close relatives within the tribes were still under obligation to carry out the divine injunction of retribution. Only further revelation of Scripture would necessarily abrogate this injunction. But the subsequent testimony of Scripture is silent in this regard. In other words, even if Genesis 9:6 were addressing a localized situation, there is no subsequent revelation, either Old Testament or New Testament, that indicates that the conditions stated in the text have changed. In any event, as was pointed out above, it is difficult to substantiate from the exegesis of Genesis 9: 1–7 that the phrase "every man's brother" refers only to siblings or near of kin.

Capital Punishment and the Noachian Covenant

In light of the context of Genesis 9:6 and the overall message of the book of Genesis, the key concept relative to capital punishment is the "image of God." This probably refers to man's relation to God as a representative who is to fulfill the goal of the Adamic commission, that is, to have dominion over the world (9:6; cf. 1:26–28). David J. A. Clines elaborates:

> That man is God's image means that he is the visible representative of the invisible, bodiless God. He is the representative rather than the representation. The image is to be understood not so much as ontologically as existentially: it comes to expression not in the nature of man so much as in his activity and function. This function is to represent God's lordship to the lower orders of creation. The dominion of man over creation can hardly be excluded from the content of the image itself.[19]

This functional interpretation of the image of God is based upon a contextual analysis of Genesis 9:6 with man's representative dominion status serving as a key component.[20] However, further analysis of the *imago Dei* which employs the structures of systematic theology reveals that there are secondary elements of the *imago Dei* as well. In other words, the function of man as image-bearer is primary in the Genesis account. The content of the image of God is secondary in the account.

In keeping with the substantive view maintained in Reformed tradition, the *imago Dei* may be described as threefold. First, the term *image* can refer to the natural endowments and spiritual qualities (e.g., true knowledge, righteousness, integrity, and holiness) that man possessed before the Fall.[21] Second, the image of God may also refer to those elements which belonged to man even after the Fall (e.g., intellectual power, natural affections or emotions, and the moral freedom to choose). It should be noted that even in his fallen state man is said to be in "the image of God" (cf. Gen. 9:6; 1 Cor. 11:7, and James 3:7–9). Third, there is the spiritual aspect of man that constitutes the *imago Dei*. That is, persons are uniquely created as spirit beings. Mankind also possesses personality, namely, character traits and attitudes that distinguish man and woman from the animal world. Humans also are characterized by consciousness, i.e., the unique capacity of self-awareness. They are also destined for immortality or endless spiritual existence.[22] In summary, the substantive view of the *imago Dei* refers to that composite unity of traits that fallen humanity shares in a limited sense with God.

The significance of the image of God to the death penalty prescribed in Genesis 9:6 is stated as follows. First, the clause "for in the image of God he made man" (v. 6c) indicates that God's original intention for man was to have dominion over the world. Through man, God's representative counterpart, the creation was to be ruled "in such a way that it [creation] would come to realize its full potential."[23] But the dominion of the earth was not for man's selfish and exploitive gain.[24] "Murder then," as described by Westermann, "is a direct attack on God's right to dominion."[25] Murder is viewed as a usurping of God's unique right to prescribe life or death.

God alone possesses the prerogative to justly enact the death sentence. But when persons violate the apodictic injunction of Genesis 9:5–6, God uses man as his dominion counterpart to bring retribution upon the guilty. Second, because man possesses the qualitative spiritual endowments in the relational likeness to God, human life is regarded as highly valuable to God. Consequently, it is an affront to God when his representative counterparts on earth are murdered. Baker expands upon this idea:

> . . . the sanctity of life is seen in man's identity with God, and it involves man in much more than the mere-temporal expression of his being—physical life. Because of this identity, the assault upon another man's physical life is deemed an assault upon God himself in Genesis 9:6.[26]

The Noachian Covenant, then, affirms the unique value of human life because each individual provides a personal expression of God's image through his or her life. When a person chooses to kill an image-bearer, then he or she is not only destroying a unique expression of that image, but is making an assault on the God whose image is therein reflected. Consequently, the just retribution for such an offense is for the perpetrator to surrender his or her expression of God's image through capital punishment.

Genesis 9:6 makes clear the punishment due the one who violates God's standard. But the question may be asked: In what way will the victim's blood be required of him? The answer comes in the second clause: "by man his blood will be shed." While there are a number of ways to take this statement[27] it is clear that punishment of the murderer is the shedding of his blood in retribution (not revenge).[28] Why is capital punishment taken as the punishment? The explanation, "for," is given in the second half of the clause—man is made in the image of God. Here we come down to the heart of the matter. When a person murders another he or she is in fact striking out in defiance at God, acting as if God is of no consequence. Not only has the murderer willfully shaken a fist at God (blasphemously). Such people have also put themselves in the place of God. God has a special claim upon mankind because his image is stamped on the individual. A murderer usurps God's rightful ownership by disposing of his victim's life by his deliberate action. Only the owner, God, has the right to decide when and how life ends. The willful killing of any individual is an act of rebellion against God's claim and is therefore an attack against God himself.

There is, of course, a difference between murder and prescribed killing. Murder would be the usurping of God's ownership, and as such, an attack on God himself. Prescribed killing is that in which God authorizes the taking of human life through properly administered capital punishment. Genesis 9:6 only makes sense with the distinction maintained between murder and prescribed killing. Prescribed killing is not usurpation because the owner is granting authority in special situations to do what he himself would do. The owner has the right to delegate authority over what he owns. The Noachian Covenant, therefore, bases capital punishment upon the unique value of human beings as individual embodiments of Yahweh's image. We will discuss the question of whether or not this covenant supports the death penalty today after considering capital punishment in the Mosaic Covenant.

Capital Punishment and the Mosaic Covenant

Exodus provides seemingly irrefutable evidence for both sides of the death penalty debate: a clear command that apparently proscribes killing and clear commands that apparently demand killing. Whenever

47

biblically literate individuals discuss capital punishment someone usually quotes Exodus 20:13, "Thou shalt not kill," or a passage such as Exodus 21:17, "Anyone who curses his father or mother must be put to death"(NIV), and the discussion trails off, for who can debate such clear commands or explain such an obvious contradiction? This reaction, however, demonstrates more ignorance about these commandments than respect for them. Many read the Bible as if each of its sentences stands on its own like a self-contained maxim. Such individuals, though sincere, ignore the larger context or setting of a given statement where the true meaning of the text is found.

Chapters 20 and 21 are both given by the same God to the same messenger, Moses, and come with the same authority. The same God who said, "Do not kill," also commands that

Anyone who attacks his father or his mother must be put to death. Anyone who kidnaps another and either sells him or still has him when he is caught must be put to death. Anyone who curses his father or mother must be put to death. (Exod. 21:15–17 NIV).

There is, it seems, a major problem here, for in one chapter God seemingly prohibits killing while in the next he commands it.

Readers who compare various English translations will quickly discover that the Hebrew verb translated "kill" in the King James Version is translated "murder" in other versions, such as the New King James Version, New English Bible, Today's English Version, and the New International Version. Other versions, such as the Revised Standard Version and the Jerusalem Bible, continue the traditional translation, so it is apparent that the Hebrew verb has a fairly wide range of acceptable translations. Such is the case.

The particular Hebrew verb, based on the root *ratsach*, is used forty-six times in the Old Testament in a variety of contexts that demonstrate its wide range of meanings. The King James Version, for example, translates it "kill" (1 Kings 21:19), "murder" (Jer. 7:9), "put to death" (Num. 35:30), and "slay" (Deut. 22:26). In addition, a number of other Hebrew verbs are also translated "kill" at one place or another in the King James Version. There are, it seems, different types of killing, and the verb *ratsach* may be used for several of them.

But what meaning is intended in Exodus 20:13? If we grant the assumption that God does not contradict himself, then the sixth commandment cannot be prohibiting killing in battle, for God himself commanded the armies of Israel to destroy the Canaanites when Joshua led the Israelite nation into the Promised Land. Although *ratsach* is sometimes used to describe unintentional killing, as in Deuteronomy 4:41–42, it is unreasonable to suppose that God is forbidding accidents. In light of Numbers 35:30 where the verb refers to sanctioned executions, it is likewise clear that he is not referring to capital punishment. However, in many passages, such as Psalm 94:4–7 and Hosea 6:9, *ratsach* refers to premeditated murder, something that is condemned throughout Scripture in the strongest of terms.

Since the meaning of Exodus 20:13 cannot be decided on linguistic grounds, it must be determined from the contextual data. The setting of this commandment is one in which killing in battle and execution for capital offense are repeatedly mandated. Yet the larger context, indeed the entire Old Testament, demonstrates a strong opposition to the malicious taking of human life, i.e., premeditated murder. Clearly, the Old Testament Law allowed for a socially and theologically sanctioned killing. Just as clearly it also recognized a forbidden killing. The term "murder" best describes this. Thus Exodus 20:13 should be translated "you shall not murder."

The Application of the Mosaic Law

The above discussion, however, is limited to the Old Testament theocracy. Exodus 20:13 prohibits murder, not killing of all kinds. Capital punishment, for example, is not ruled out by the sixth commandment. However, one may grant that the Old Testament Law sanctioned capital punishment without extending that sanction to the present. Two schools of thought diverge at this point. Opponents of capital punishment usually argue that the theocratic sanction behind the death penalty ended at the Cross. Just as Christ's sacrifice ended the Old Testament sacrificial system so it also ended the divine sanction of capital punishment. The death penalty was applied under the Law but cannot be applied today for there is no Law in effect. This is the view of many opponents of capital punishment, and we will devote the next chapter to a discussion of this view.

Others, however argue that the entire Old Testament theocratic law, especially capital punishment, should be applied to the contemporary world. They argue that all societies, not just the church and/or Israel, are accountable to God for obedience to the Mosaic Code in all its judicial details. The death of Christ ended the sacrificial aspect of the Mosaic Law, they argue, but the legislative requirements continue unabated as God's standard for all societies everywhere. These individuals, often termed "reconstructionists" or "theonomists," argue for the death penalty and extend its application to all actions identified as capital crimes by the Old Testament Law.[29] It is our contention that their approach is fatally flawed.

While we are in agreement with these individuals on the divine sanction of capital punishment for today, we reject their arguments. They have come to the right conclusion for the wrong reasons. Cessation of the Mosaic Code does not mark the end of the death penalty, nor does that Code have to continue in order to validate capital punishment.

Several observations show that the Mosaic Law has, in fact, ended. First of all, it is our contention that the Mosaic Covenant with its commandments, statutes, and judgments was given to Israel to codify the expected conduct of a nation uniquely related to God. Moses' rehearsal of God's dealings with Israel in his song (Deut. 32) reveals the uniqueness of Israel and the distinction between God's dealings with Israel and his dealings with other nations. We agree with Calvin regarding the Sinaitic (Mosaic) Law:

> For the statement of some, that the Law of God given through Moses is dishonored when it is abrogated and new laws preferred to it, is utterly vain. For others are not preferred to it when they are more approved, not by a simple comparison, but with regard to the condition of times, place, and nation or when that law is abrogated which was never enacted for us. For the Lord through the hand of Moses did not give that law to be proclaimed among all nations and to be in force everywhere; but when he had taken the Jewish nation into his safekeeping, defense, and protection, he also willed to be a lawgiver especially to it and—as became a wise lawgiver—he had special concern for it in making its laws.[30]

The unique relationship that Israel enjoyed with Yahweh is termed a "covenant" (Exod.19:5), the key word in God's revealed relationships with mankind. It is the basic means for administrating God's rule on the earth.[31] Mendenhall defines covenant as "a solemn promise made binding by an oath, which may be either a verbal formula or a symbolic action."[32] Others focus on the idea of obligation or legal contract.[33] A covenant could be between individuals or between nations, it could be between equals, or imposed by a superior on an inferior. It was essentially a contract, treaty or bond which bound the parties to certain obligations to one another. Theologically, God's relationship with man and man's obligations to God are always described in covenantal terms. Hence "covenant" becomes the central organizing principle of the Old Testament apart from which ethics cannot be correctly understood.

Essentially, three types of covenant forms were used in the Old Testament: the suzerain-vassal treaty, the royal grant treaty, and the parity treaty. No matter which type of treaty or covenant is discussed they all partake of certain characteristic elements. All of these elements are not contained in every treaty, neither do they all follow this order. The major difference between the parity and the suzerain treaty is that the superior in the suzerain treaty coerced the vassal into accepting the terms of the treaty while his obligations were only voluntarily subscribed to. The suzerain treaty obligated the servant to the master, whereas the royal grant was a voluntary obligation of the master to the servant. The elements of the suzerain-vassal treaty are:

1. The preamble, which identifies the king or treaty participants.

2. The historical prologue which describes the previous relationships between the two parties.

3. The stipulations, which outlines the obligations of the treaty.

4. The deposit and public reading of the treaty.

5. The list of witnesses, usually before the God or gods.

6. The blessings and curses.[34]

When Moses had brought the people to Mt. Sinai, God called him into his presence and began to institute a unique covenant with Israel which bound Israel to God as vassal to the Great King. Israel is now said to be distinguished from the rest of the nations in three statements. First, they would be a special possession to God above all the nations. The Hebrew for "possession" indicates a treasure or property that has been reserved or carefully put aside for personal use.[35] This indicates that the relationship of Israel to Yahweh is similar to that of the vassal. Their position with respect to the rest of the nations as separate and distinct is highlighted by the Hebrew preposition used which signifies separation.

The ground of this is given in a phrase sometimes overlooked, "for all the earth is mine." Here God states that all the earth is his and the special place of Israel will serve the larger purposes of the Abrahamic Covenant, to bring world-wide redemption. This assertion of God's universal sovereignty is a reminder that he is still the sovereign or suzerain over all the world which is viewed in some sense still as his servant, but Israel will be his servant in a unique way to bring redemption to the whole.

Second, Israel would be a kingdom of priests. A priest had a unique function as a mediator between God and men. So Israel would now have a unique mediatorial role between God and the rest of the nations. Their role thenceforth would be to mediate or intercede as priests between the holy God and the wayward nations of the world, with the end in view not only of declaring his salvation, but of providing the human channel in and through whom that salvation would be effected.[36] Third, Israel would be a holy nation.[37] This is not "holy" in the sense of morally pure, but in the sense of a nation set apart to God for a particular purpose. These two designations seem to be synonymous. Israel is viewed now not just as a collection of descendants from Abraham, but as a distinct entity with a distinct and unique function within the plan of God. Thus these two terms describe Israel's function within the confines of the Abrahamic Covenant. As God worked his redemptive plan out in history, he chose to work in a special way through a specific people.

It is in these critical verses that covenantal discontinuity is established between Israel and the rest of the nations. The structure of Exodus 20–23 clearly borrows from the suzerain-vassal treaty form and shows at the very least that Israel is a unique vassal of Yahweh. The ethical stipulations laid out there are clearly for Israel as a distinct people already in a covenant relationship with Yahweh and cannot be dealt with apart from this context. This new covenant revealed to Israel is clearly for Israel alone and not for the other nations. It is clearly a description of the type of life that a "kingdom of priests" should have.

The Ten Commandments and the judgments in Exodus 20–33 are an explanation of how covenant people are to live. The keeping of the Sinaitic Law was the outward expression of a relationship that had been established prior to the covenant and was not the prerequisite for the covenant. Thus grace preceded the giving of the Law. This is in contrast to Rushdoony's claim that law is the framework for grace.[38] These stipulations were not for mankind in general, but for Israel who, by means of the Abrahamic Covenant and the Exodus event now stood in a state of grace. The Mosaic Law merely explicated the type of life that must be lived if the covenant relationship was going to be fully enjoyed. This meant that the Law of the Sinaitic Covenant was not merely abstract legislation or ethical standard, but was guidance or instruction for life within the framework of an already established, unique relationship with Yahweh.

Throughout the Old Testament, God affirms that the Sinaitic Covenant was strictly for Israel. Deuteronomy 4:6–8 describes the impact Israel's obedience to the statutes and judgments would have on the surrounding nations:

> Therefore be careful to observe them for this is your wisdom and your understanding in the sight of the peoples who will hear all these statutes, and say, "Surely this great nation is a wise and understanding people." (NASB)

It is our contention that the Sinaitic Covenant with its commandments, statutes, and judgments was given to Israel to codify the expected conduct of a nation uniquely related to God.

The Noachian Covenant and Civil Government

If the Mosaic Law has no direct application to contemporary society, is there any support for capital punishment in the Old Testament? We affirm that there is, and that it is found in the Noachian rather than the Mosaic Covenant. Since, as we have already argued, the terms of the Noachian Covenant must be understood as universal in scope, the next question involves the relationship of the covenant to human government. Most conservative commentators have understood that

God is establishing a new principle in the covenant by giving mankind a degree of responsibility for self-government. This means that this covenant marks the start of human government.

In the classic theological literature, both Reformed and Dispensational, it is generally recognized that Genesis 9:1–7 institutes a new era of responsibility for mankind.[39] This new era is often called "civil government," or "human government." Though the context of Genesis 9: 1–7 is addressed to Noah and his sons, it is clear that the injunction of Genesis 9:5–6 serves as a seed-plot for the emerging and the more fully developed law system that was later instituted at Sinai for the nation Israel. With regard to Genesis 9:6 as the point of origin of the universal institution of human government, Luther's comments are appropriate:

> Here we have the source from which stem all civil law and the law of nations. If God grants to man power over life and death, surely he also grants power over what is less, such as property, the home, wife, children, servants, and fields. All these God wants to be subject to the power of certain human beings, in order that they may punish the guilty . . . . If God had not conferred this divine power on men, what sort of life do you suppose we would be living? Because He foresaw that there would be always a great abundance of evil men, He established this outward remedy . . . in order that wantonness might not increase beyond measure. With this hedge, these walls, God has given protection for our life and possessions.[40]

In the same way, James emphasizes the need for a required act of civil justice according to the strictures of Genesis 9:6:

> . . . the power of the sword is the cutting edge of authority necessary for an effective civil government. This is true because directives issued by civil government are not enforceable except when accomplished by the threat of sanctions—the raw power necessary to coerce obedience from the unwilling subjects. In particular, civil government is obligated to function as God's agent of retribution by punishing (with death) those who unjustly kill other human beings. Thus, justice is brought upon murderers, and some (secondary) deterrent effect is gained against the proliferation of violence which typified life upon the earth prior to the Noahic flood.[41]

In addition to the foregoing discussion, there are at least two general implications for modern civil human government that follow from the Genesis 9:6 mandate. First, every murder demands just punishment, punishment that is proportionate to the crime. Second, because man was made in the image of God, to destroy man is a crime against God. Therefore, God appoints man to carry out the death penalty upon murderers who attempt to usurp his established order.

In regard to the second point above, it is observed from New Testament revelation that the Genesis 9:6 mandate is still in effect for society today. A central passage in this connection is Romans 13:3–4: "For rulers are not a cause of fear for good behavior, but for evil. Do you want to have no fear of authority? Do what is good, and you will have praise from the same; for it is a minister of God to you for good. But if you do what is evil, be afraid for it does not bear the sword for nothing; for it is a minister of God, an avenger who brings wrath upon the one who practices evil" (NASB).

This passage contains two important features that are tied directly to the Genesis 9:6 mandate. First, because civil government is "a minister of God," a continuing permanent relationship exists between God and human governments. Second, as Steven James puts it, commenting on Romans 13, "government performs its ministerial function by acting for God as retributive agent—to reward those who do good and to bring wrath upon those who do evil."[42] Other New Testament texts are consonant with this idea of governmental authority serving as a divinely appointed retributive agency (e.g., John 19:11; Acts 25:10–12; 1 Tim. 2:1–2; 1 Pet. 2:13–14). Consequently, even though capital punishment for non-homicidal offenses committed under the Mosaic Law has been abrogated through the finished work of Christ, it is at the same time recognized that New Testament revelation has not obliterated the Genesis 9:6 mandate.

Conclusion

Genesis 9:6 is part of the covenant God made with Noah following the Deluge. This covenant, made with the entire human race, establishes, among other things, the principle of capital punishment for murder. The death penalty is to be exercised as a governmental

55

function, not as an item of personal revenge. Capital punishment is based upon the unique value of individual human beings because they bear the image of God. The context of Genesis 9:6 shows that it is to be applied to all of mankind, not a limited group. Further, the passage is definitely prescriptive, for it describes a specific penalty that will be assessed for a specific crime. Genesis 9:6 teaches that capital punishment is a proper penalty that governments may apply in the case of premeditated murder.

The Old Testament supports capital punishment today, at least in the case of murder, through the Noachian Covenant, the last covenant to be established with all humanity, and the only covenant still in universal effect.

NOTES

1. Not all accept this interpretation of Genesis 9:6.

2. In view of the subsequent distinction between premeditated and accidental killing found in the Mosaic Law, we will assume that the murder involved in this passage is premeditated and not accidental.

3. Allen Ross, *Creation and Blessing: A Guide to the Study and Exposition of Genesis* (Grand Rapids, Mich.: Baker Book House, 1988), 201.

4. Lloyd R. Bailey, *Capital Punishment: What the Bible Says*, 34–35; see bibliography.

5. William H. Baker, *Worthy of Death*, 102; see bibliography.

6. Ibid., 134.

7. Ibid., 134–35.

8. See A. B. Rhodes, "Bible and Capital Punishment," *Eternity* 12 (June 1961): 17–18; John Howard Yoder, "Capital Punishment and the Bible," *Christianity Today* 4 (February 1969): 5.

9. Rhodes, 17–18.

10. Baker, 143–44.

11. Charles Spear, a nineteenth-century death penalty opponent argued this position. James J. Megivern, "Biblical Arguments in the Capital Punishment Debate," *Perspectives in Religious Studies* 8 (1981): 143–53.

12. Malcom A. Reid, "Does Genesis 9 Justify Capital Punishment? No," in *The Genesis Debate*, ed. Ronald Youngblood (New York: Thomas Nelson, 1986), 243.

13. Claus Westermann, *Genesis 1–11: A Commentary*, trans. John J. Scullion (Minneapolis: Augsburg Publishing House, 1984), 467–68. Apodictic law differs from causative law. The latter serves to give a particular instance, and then the resultant ruling. It is usually stated as an *If . . . Then* formula. See R. A. Cole, "Law in the Old Testament," in Volume 3 of *The Zondervan Pictorial Encyclopedia of the Bible* (Grand Rapids: Zondervan Publishing House, 1975).

14. Bailey, 39.

15. Baker, 84.

16. Lewis B. Smedes, "Is the Death Penalty Necessary?" *United Evangelical Action* (December 1964): 14.

17. Ibid.

18. Steven A. James, "Divine Justice and the Retributive Duty of Civil Government," *Trinity Journal* 6 (1985): 205.

19. David J. A. Clines, "The Image of God in Man," *Tyndale Bulletin* 19 (1968): 101.

20. See the excellent discussions provided in Gunnlaugur A. Johsson, *The Image of God: Genesis 1:26–28 in a Century of Old Testament Research* (Stockholm: Almqvist & Wiksell International, 1988); and Millard J. Erickson, *Christian Theology* (Grand Rapids: Baker Book House, 1984), 495–517.

21. Louis Berkhof, *Systematic Theology*, 4th ed. (Grand Rapids, Mich.: Wm. B. Eerdmans Publishing Co., 1969), 202–203. Berkhof provides the historical differences between Luther's and Calvin's interpretations of the image of God.

22. Ibid., 205.

23. Erickson, 510.

24. Ibid.

25. Claus Westermann, *Genesis 1–11*, 468.

26. Baker, 39–40.

27. This could be interpreted as descriptive rather than prescriptive, for example.

28. I distinguish between retribution, which is just punishment or payment for a crime, thus using a standard of righteousness, and arbitrariness which is based on emotion or individual perspective. I use revenge as an individual striking out at another for a perceived wrong which may have no justification at law.

29. For further reading on the theonomist view, see two books by Greg L. Bahnsen, *By This Standard: The Authority of God's Law Today* (Tyler, Tex.: Institute for Christian Economics, 1985), and *Theonomy in Christian Economics* (Phillipsburg, N. J.: The Presbyterian and Reformed Publishing Co., 1973).

30. J ohn Calvin, Institutes of the Christian Religion in John T. McNeil, ed., *The Library of Christian Classics* (Philadelphia: Westminster Press, 1960), 21 (Book IV, xx. 16).

31. Recent evangelical perspectives on covenant can be found in William J. Dumbrell, *Covenant and Creation* (Nashville: Thomas Nelson, 1984); O. Palmer Robertson, *Christ and the Covenants* (Phillipsburg: Presbyterian and Reformed Publishing Company, 1980); Thomas Edward McComiskey, *The Covenants of Promise* (Grand Rapids, Mich.: Baker Book House, 1985).

32. George Mendenhall, "Covenant," *International Dictionary of the Bible* (Nashville: Abingdon, 1962), 1:714.

33. Eugene H. Merrill, "Covenant and the Kingdom: Genesis 1–3 as Foundation for Biblical Theology," *Criswell Theological Review* 1 (1987): 296.

34. Mendenhall, "Covenant," p. 714.

35. F. Brown, S. R. Driver, and C. A. Briggs, *Hebrew and English Lexicon of the Old Testament* (Oxford: Clarendon Press, 1907), 688.

36. Eugene H. Merrill, *Kingdom of Priests* (Grand Rapids, Mich.: Baker Book House, 1988), 80.

37. Nation here is *goy*, a word rarely used of Israel, but it is used here and in the Abrahamic Covenant in Genesis 1:22. Thus usage here is reminiscent of the Abrahamic Covenant.

38. R. J. Rushdoony, *The Institutes of Biblical Law* (Nutley, N. J.: Craig Press, 1973), 75.

39. Martin Luther, "Lectures in Genesis," in *Works of Martin Luther* (Philadelphia: Muhlenberg, 1931), 2:140–41.

40. Ibid.

41. James, 204–205.

42. Ibid.

4

The New Testament and Capital Punishment

The teachings of Jesus Christ and the apostle Paul provide the theological foundation for New Testament Christianity. Those of us who call ourselves Christians must evaluate our lives from this perspective. There is no question that God commanded capital punishment as part of the Noachian Covenant, nor should there be any debate that the death penalty was part of the Mosaic Covenant. Things, however, were changed after the death, burial, and resurrection of Jesus Christ. If his redemptive work on the Cross changed the application of other aspects of the Old Testament, such as sacrifices, then perhaps he also set aside capital punishment as a legitimate form of punishment. Many think that Jesus and Paul have done exactly this. If true, then the debate is settled. We, however, are convinced that neither Jesus nor Paul abrogated capital punishment. This chapter will examine the Gospels and the Epistles to ascertain the position each held on the death penalty.

The Teachings of Jesus Christ

Clearly the cross-work of Jesus Christ brought about major changes in the relationship of man and God, and none so dramatic as the place

59

of the Mosaic Law in the life of the New Testament believer. Christ ended the sacrificial system (Heb. 10:1–18), unified believing Jew and Gentile into one body (Eph. 2:11–22), and freed believers from the judicial authority of the Law (Rom. 7:1–6, Col. 2:16–23). Not only this, but during his earthly ministry he challenged the very foundation of Jewish traditionalism, ridiculing the Jewish authorities for their neglect of justice, mercy, and faithfulness:

> Woe to you, teachers of the law and Pharisees, you hypocrites! You give a tenth of your spices—mint, dill and cummin. But you have neglected the more important matters of the law—justice, mercy and faithfulness. You should have practiced the latter, without neglecting the former. You blind guides! You strain out a gnat but swallow a camel. (Matt. 23:23–24 NIV)

In light of this, what changes did Jesus make in the rules of capital punishment? Did he set aside the Mosaic Law or the Noachian Covenant with their emphasis upon retributive punishment, including the death penalty for murder, and replace them with another concept, one based on love and forgiveness? Or did he acknowledge the legitimacy of capital punishment and permit its practice? Although Jesus gave no direct statement on the subject, it is possible to gain an understanding of his position by analyzing three key passages: the Sermon on the Mount, the story of the woman taken in adultery, and his own response to his trials and execution.

Some, however, object to using specific passages to determine Jesus' mind on a given topic. They would rather seek the general tenor of his thinking by looking at the overall content of the Gospels. "It is not what the Bible says in a specific verse, but what it says to us through its total message, interpreted in terms of our own conditions, that is relevant."[1]

The concept sounds valid, but we wonder how to obtain the total message of Christ without studying specific passages which describe what he said and did? Moreover, how is one to guard against the natural tendency to identify the readers' own mind with that of Jesus? Sometimes those who seek the mind of Jesus ignore passages which seem to contradict their preconceived view of the subject. Certain texts are likely

60

to be ruled out of court, since they do not fit the image of a patient, loving, forgiving Lord:

> Physically beating those with whom he disagreed (John 2:13–15); berating those religious leaders who disagreed with him by calling them children "of hell" (Matt. 23:15) who deserve to be sentenced to that place (Matt. 23:29–33); designated the Jews (of which he was a part) carte blanche as children of "the devil" (John 8:44); announced that any place which will not receive his disciples will fare worse than Sodom and Gomorrah (Matt. 10:14–15); responding to a mother's plea for her sick child by telling her that "it is not right to take the children's bread and throw it to the dogs" (i.e., to foreigners, Mark 7:24–27); constantly berating his disciples (e.g., Mark 8:17–18), and even those in need of his help (Mark 9:19); etc.[2]

Our study of capital punishment in the mind of Christ will of necessity center on specific passages in which we find him interacting with the death penalty in his culture. These sections will be the basis for our conclusions.

When we open the New Testament we find a world radically changed from that of the Old. Though the Jewish nation had religious freedom, Palestine was ruled by the Roman Empire. Rome, a Gentile power, was the dominant political and military authority. Judaism had become encrusted with a traditionalism so thick that little of its original light shined forth. Into this context came the Messiah, proclaiming his radical message of repentance and renewal to the Jewish people. He did not come to prophetically hold Rome accountable to God through the Mosaic Covenant. In fact, he commanded his disciples to avoid both the Samaritans and the Gentiles in their preaching (Matt. 10:5). Consequently Jesus said little about the political authority of Rome and its exercise of capital punishment. He acknowledged Caesar's general authority, but did not elaborate on its specific exercise (cf. Matthew 22:21). Consequently we must analyze his personal teachings to his people for insights into his view of capital punishment. Here we also find that he said nothing specific about the death penalty, but it is possible to draw some conclusions about it from his other teachings.

THE DEATH PENALTY DEBATE

The Sermon on the Mount

In the Sermon on the Mount (Matt. 5–7), Jesus attacked the traditionalism which prevented an accurate understanding of the Mosaic Law and hindered its correct application to the lives of his audience. In this context, he gave the teaching which is most frequently quoted in the capital punishment debate:

> You have heard that it was said, "Love your neighbor and hate your enemy." But I tell you: Love your enemies and pray for those who persecute you, that you may be sons of your Father in heaven. . . . Be perfect, therefore, as your heavenly Father is perfect. (Matt. 5:43–44, 48 NIV).

The first phrase he cites, "love your neighbor," comes from Leviticus 19:18, "Do not seek revenge or bear a grudge against one of your people, but love your neighbor as yourself. I am the Lord." The second phrase does not come from the Old Testament but reflects the traditionalism of his day and the general tendency of sinful humanity. Jesus is not rejecting the Mosaic teaching, but showing his listeners that the life lived in obedience to the Law goes beyond normal expectations. This is in perfect agreement with Leviticus 19:17, "Do not hate your brother in your heart" (also cited in Matthew 5:22). Jesus' call, therefore, is for "mature action in the day-to-day events of ordinary life: to be without prejudice and devoid of self-interested motives."[3]

The entire passage as well as its context centers on personal responses to difficult situations. Jesus' concern is the attitude more than the act: hate more than murder (5:21–24), sexual desire more than adultery (5:27–30), love of enemies rather than hate for them (5:43–48). None of this contradicts any part of the Mosaic Law. Jesus refocuses the Law on the personal lives of his listeners rather than rejects or replaces it with new teaching (5:17–20).

None of his teaching is directed to the governmental authorities of his day. In fact, Jesus acknowledged the existence of courts and councils without rejecting their validity (5:25–26). His commands only "limit the believer's response in these situations to what love and Scriptures impose."[4] There is nothing in the Sermon on the Mount that challenges capital punishment as a part of existing governmental practices, Jewish or Roman. If, as some claim, we had to be perfect to exercise punishment (cf. 5:48), then all punishment for any sin would be eliminated and anarchy would reign supreme. Matthew 5:43–48 does not eliminate the validity of capital punishment.

Matthew 5:21–22, on the other hand, shows that Jesus recognized that murder merits judgment. Certainly he knew that Exodus 20:13 prohibited murder, and that Exodus 21:12 commanded the death penalty for the crime. Yet, Jesus said nothing against such a judgment. In fact, he built upon its severity to warn against the attitude of hatred in the strongest of terms. If the Sermon on the Mount shows us anything about Jesus' attitude toward capital punishment, it shows us that he accepted it as a valid exercise of governmental authority and a proper part of the Mosaic Code.

The Woman Taken in Adultery[5]

Adultery was a capital offense according to the Mosaic Law, so when the Pharisees brought a woman to Jesus who had been caught in that very act, he looked capital punishment right in the face (John 8:1–11). Those who oppose the death penalty argue that his refusal to condemn the woman shows that Jesus rejected capital punishment in favor of a higher ideal.

> With sovereign authority Jesus transcended the law and demonstrated the grace of God in the forgiveness of sins. His practice like his teaching was based on his conception of God. He had not come to carry out punishment according to legal requirements or exact proper revenge, but to seek the lost, to redeem the ungodly and to reconcile sinners to God.[6]

The argument sounds impressive, especially in light of the radical nature of Jesus' ministry, but it is open to serious, indeed, fatal objections.

The real issue placed before Jesus was not a guilty woman but a baited trap (8:6). Both Pharisees and Messiah knew that Leviticus 20:10 and Deuteronomy 22:22–24 required that the woman guilty of adultery be executed, whether she was married or not. Both Pharisees and Messiah knew that the Law required the testimony of two or three witnesses before conviction. And both Pharisee and Messiah knew that Roman law reserved the right of capital punishment for itself. If Jesus had agreed to her execution, then he would have been guilty of rebellion against Rome.[7] If, however, he waffled on the death penalty, then he would be rebelling against the Mosaic Code. His unexpected response disarmed the accusers and his mercy freed the woman: "If any one of you is without sin, let him be the first to throw a stone at her," and, "Neither do I condemn you . . . go now and leave your life of sin" (8:11). Does Jesus also disarm the death penalty and free humanity from its curse?

If Jesus is both rebuking the Pharisees and rejecting capital punishment, then it is clear that he is dealing only with a specific situation: adultery. The passage cannot be extended to include murder, since that crime is covered by the Mosaic and the Noachian Covenants.[8] It is also clear that Jesus is not demanding complete sinlessness of every witness, jury member, and judge, for then the criminal justice system would not be possible at all. This is inconsistent with the New Testament's general affirmation of judicial sanctions as a demonstration of divine justice (cf. Rom. 13:1–7). What, then, did Jesus do that so effectively silenced his opponents?

The Pharisees were half-right: Leviticus 20:10 and Deuteronomy 22:22–24 demanded the execution of a woman taken in adultery. But the Law also required the execution of the man as well, and the woman's partner was notably absent. Presumably the witnesses saw his sin as well as that of the woman since she was, after all, taken in the very act (8:4). The witnesses, then, were equally guilty of breaking the Law and, according to Deuteronomy 19:16–21, were also guilty of a capital crime.

> The sense . . . is that the scribes and Pharisees were not *without fault* as witnesses in such a judicial proceeding, because they themselves were guilty of violating the provisions of Deuteronomy 22:22–24. Stricken in conscience, the hypocritical witnesses left the scene, and Jesus dismissed the case when no one remained to press charges. Far from abrogating the provisions of the Mosaic law, Jesus demonstrated that he took their procedural guidelines for the protection of accused persons very seriously. This understanding of Jesus'

action in this pericope is consistent with his statement in Matthew 5:17 that he did not come to abolish the law of Moses, but to fulfill it.[9]

Capital punishment never became an issue for Jesus. As for the woman, who else could forgive sins except the Lawgiver himself (cf. Luke 5:20–25)? Consequently, this passage does not prove that Jesus intended to abolish the death penalty either in general or for the specific crime of adultery. Arguments against capital punishment must appeal to texts other than this one.

Other Passages

When Pilate warned him that he had "the power either to free you or to crucify you" (John 19:10), Jesus acknowledged the reality of Pilate's authority, but pointed him toward its true source: "You would have no power over me if it were not given to you from above" (John 19:11). Jesus recognized that Pilate's authority as the governing official came from God and that it was being manipulated by others for an unjust end ("The one who handed me over to you is guilty of a greater sin"). However, the validity of Pilate's authority to execute Jesus was never questioned by either.

Jesus also appealed to pre-Mosaic decrees to settle arguments, decrees that were given to the whole of humanity, not just Israel. The basis for marriage is not the Mosaic Law, but the decree of Genesis (cf. Matt. 19:3–9). Jesus did not specifically speak of the Noachian Covenant, but neither did he reject it. The fact that he recognized that pre-Mosaic decrees were still valid even under the Mosaic Law, however, supports our previous contention that the Noachian Covenant was still operative during the theocracy, and is still in effect today.

Summary

Throughout his life Jesus obeyed the Mosaic Code and, as Messiah to Israel, demanded obedience to its precepts. He refocused its demands upon the attitudes of its adherents, not just their acts. When confronted by hypocritical, false witnesses he exposed them for what they were

65

and extended mercy to the guilty. We conclude, therefore, that Jesus accepted the Mosaic Code, complete with capital punishment, and did nothing, by word or deed, to abrogate the death penalty.

The Teachings of The Apostles

Most of the apostolic writings in the New Testament deal with ecclesiastical concerns and touch on the world only when the church is directly involved. Consequently, we do not find the apostles giving any direct statements concerning capital punishment. As with Jesus, we must find their answer to our question by drawing it out of what they said and did.

The New Testament records the detailed response of only one apostle when confronted with execution—Paul. When Festus offered him a chance to go to Jerusalem for trial, a trip on which he would probably have been ambushed, Paul appealed to Caesar, claiming,

> I have not done any wrong to the Jews, as you yourself know very well. If, however, I am guilty of doing anything deserving death, I do not refuse to die." (Acts 25:10–11 NIV)

Two things stand out in this affirmation. First, Paul presumably considered some crimes worthy of death. These are not specified, of course, but his recognition of capital crime runs counter to those who try to employ his teachings to argue against capital punishment. The second point is that Paul did not question Rome's authority to execute him. He claimed the protection afforded him by Roman law, and he also accepted its authority to execute him if a capital crime were involved. This evidence, though circumstantial, argues that Paul accepted the validity of capital punishment.

Only two passages from the Epistles speak to the issue of governmental authority: 1 Peter 2:13–14 and Romans 13:1–7. The Petrine passage, the more general of the two, simply admonishes believers to

> submit yourselves for the Lord's sake to every authority instituted among men: whether to the king, as the supreme authority, or to

governors, who are sent by him to punish those who do wrong and to commend those who do right. (NIV)

Peter says nothing about capital punishment, but if other passages show that God has placed the death penalty within governmental authority, then the believer has no option but to accept it. We must look to Paul to see whether capital punishment is still part of governmental authority.

The second passage, Romans 13:1–7, is the determinative one insofar as capital punishment is concerned, and therefore will be examined in detail. Paul discussed many theological points in Romans other than the role of human government. Throughout this epistle and many of his others, Paul affirmed that the Mosaic Code had ended as the judicial measuring stick for the believer's life. The Law had been fulfilled on the Cross, and a new way was open for the believers to approach God. Romans 7, Galatians 3–4, Ephesians 2, and Colossians 2 are major sections in which Paul discusses the believers' new relationship to God and to each other as the result of the sacrifice of Jesus Christ.

It would seem reasonable, then, to infer that the capital punishment provisions of the Mosaic Code had also been set aside. No longer would someone be executed for breaking the Sabbath, adultery, cursing parents, etc. The Law was over, and with it went the commands that outlined capital crimes and the death penalty. Paul knew this, but nowhere does he affirm that the death penalty is invalid. Nowhere does he state that capital punishment has been abrogated in the New Testament economy. It is also true that he nowhere directly affirms the validity of capital punishment, either, although his response to Festus points in that direction.

With the end of the Mosaic Code before him, Paul commanded submission to human government because that institution was established by God and carries out essential functions on behalf of God in this world.

Ryrie identifies four principles affirmed by Paul in Romans 13:1–7:

(1) Human government is ordained by God (v. 1), yet it is a sphere of authority that is distinct from others like that of the home or the church; (2) human government is to be obeyed by the Christian

because it is of God, because it opposes evil (v. 4), and because our consciences tell us to obey (v. 5); (3) the government has the right of taxation (vv. 6–7); and (4) the government has the right to use force (v. 4).[10]

The context of this passage is instructive in appreciating the importance of the principles Ryrie has identified. In Romans 12:17–21, Paul commands believers not to repay evil with evil, to give up personal revenge, to make room for God's wrath, and to overcome evil with good. God, according to Paul, will take care of justice. The personal responsibility of the Christian is to exercise patience, act in love, and get out of God's way so that he can exercise his wrath in vengeance (cf. Lev. 19:18). But how will God accomplish this if the individual believer does nothing to obtain vengeance on his own? The answer, of course, is human government.

This is why Paul identifies governmental authorities as agents of "God's wrath," for they are authorized by God to do what individual believers are prohibited from doing: exercising God's wrath on sin through judicial actions. Romans 13:1–7 answers the "how" of Romans 12:17–21. God's judicial wrath is exercised through human government. We are not implying that all governments are perfect, that all governments properly punish evil and reward good, nor that all governments should be obeyed. We are affirming that God has established human governments as his agents to punish sin on this earth, regardless of whether they properly carry out this mandate.

The establishment of human government obviously antedated the Mosaic Code and when the Law ended at the Cross, human government continued with God's blessing. As we have seen, the first reference to human government, that is, judicial authority, is Genesis 9:6. Here God gives mankind judicial authority to exercise his wrath for the sin of murder, and he establishes the death penalty as punishment for that crime. The obvious question, then, is whether contemporary governments still have God's authorization to exercise capital punishment.

Paul speaks of a governmental "sword" (*machaira*), and his statement has been given widely differing interpretations. Some affirm that it is a clear reference to the instrument of decapitation and thus affirmation of capital punishment.[11] Others look at it as a symbolic reference to the use of force, much like the policeman's club and pistol today.[12] The sword, however, appears to be a significant item in the magistrate's arsenal. Therefore, the reference seems to go beyond the merely symbolic to the actual use of the instrument. This does not prove, however, that Paul is affirming the death penalty, but his terminology is far closer to an affirmation than a denial.

To exclude the right of the death penalty when the nature of the crime calls for such is totally contrary to that which the sword signifies and executes. The usage of the sword in the New Testament connotes death (Matt. 26:52, Luke 21:21, Acts 12:2, 16:27; Heb. 11:34, 37; Rev. 13:10).[13] Therefore, we conclude that Romans 13:1–7 endorses capital punishment as a valid option for contemporary governments in their exercise of divine wrath against sin.

Conclusion

The biblical evidence for capital punishment may be summarized with these observations. In Genesis 9 God establishes a covenant with all humanity in which, among other things, he gives mankind permission to exercise judicial authority among themselves to exercise his wrath against the crime of murder. The established penalty for this act is death. The Mosaic Covenant established, among other things, the rules and regulations by which the descendants of Abraham would live as those under the Abrahamic Covenant. Those rules mandated capital punishment for a number of crimes, including murder. While the laws of the Mosaic Covenant, including those of capital punishment, are no longer binding in the New Testament economy, the provisions of the Noachian Covenant are still in force. This covenant provides capital punishment for the crime of murder today. Nothing in the teachings of Jesus or the apostles contradicts this sanctioning. Capital punishment is a proper course of action for governments today in the exercise of their divine mandate to punish evil.

NOTES

1. Charles S. Milligan, "A Protestant's View of the Death Penalty," in *The Death Penalty in America*, 175–82; see bibliography.

2. Lloyd R. Bailey, *Capital Punishment: What the Bible Says*, 82; see bibliography.

3. Bailey, 74.

4. D. A. Carson, "Matthew," in *The Expositor's Bible Commentary*, vol. 8, ed. Frank Gaebelein (Grand Rapids, Mich.: Zondervan Publishing House, 1984), 156–57.

5. Many leading textual critics reject this pericope as being a part of the New Testament canon, as the marginal note in the New International Version demonstrates. For purposes of this discussion, we will treat the passage as part of the New Testament.

6. J. Arthur Hoyles, *Punishment in the Bible* (London: Epworth Press, 1986), 56.

7. On occasion Roman authorities looked the other way when the Jews independently executed people, as in the case of Stephen.

8. See Chapter 3.

9. John Jefferson Davis, *Evangelical Ethics: Issues Facing the Church Today* (Philipsburg, N.J.: Presbyterian and Reformed Publishing Co., 1985), 200.

10. Charles C. Ryrie, "The Doctrine of Capital Punishment," *Bibliotheca Sacra* (July, 1972): 216.

11. William G. T. Shedd, *A Critical and Doctrinal Commentary Upon the Epistle of St. Paul to the Romans*, (New York: Charles Scribner's Sons, 1879), 328.

12. C. E. B. Cranfield, *The Epistle of Romans*, in the *International Critical Commentary Series*, vol. 2 (Edinburgh: T & T Clark, 1979), 667.

13. John Murray, *The Epistle to the Romans* (Grand Rapids, Mich.: Wm. B. Eerdmans Publishing Co., 1968), 152–53.

5

The Moral Arguments
For Capital Punishment

Despite the fact that the Bible clearly teaches the validity of capital punishment, many today oppose it on moral grounds. They argue that the death penalty in any form is immoral, in that it violates basic standards of both private and public morality. No person or organization has any right to take the life of a human being, regardless of his or her actions. Our modern sense of justice, some argue, has advanced beyond the crude, revenge-oriented mentality of past centuries, and we no longer need to continue the cycle of violence through executions. For example, former United States Deputy Attorney General Ramsey Clark stated that

> this nation is so great in its resources and too good in its purposes to engage in the light of recent understanding in the deliberate taking of human life as either a punishment or a deterrent to domestic crime.[1]

United States Supreme Court Justice William Brennan claims that the death penalty is inconsistent with human dignity because it treats "members of the human race as nonhumans, as objects to be toyed with and discarded."[2] These arguments seem to eliminate the death penalty, especially in light of God's standards of morality. However, there are sound answers to them which will be explored in this chapter. We will show that capital punishment as a retributive punishment is not only moral, but is a moral imperative according to God's established order.

The Moral Case for Capital Punishment

A person's ethics depends upon one's philosophical presuppositions and, for the Christian, one's view of biblical authority. There can be no true light on any subject from the Christian viewpoint without considering the teachings of Scripture on the subject. This is especially true when questions of morality are involved. Consequently, we will construct this part of our defense of capital punishment from a biblical perspective.

Capital Punishment Respects the Imago Dei

The Bible, as we have seen, teaches that mankind sustains a unique relationship to God because he bears the *imago Dei*. The importance of this concept cannot be overemphasized. Carl F. H. Henry has perceptibly described the significance of the phrase, "the image of God":

> The importance of a proper understanding of the *imago Dei* can hardly be overstated. The answer given to the *imago* inquiry soon becomes determinative for the entire gamut of doctrinal affirmation. The ramifications are not only theological, but affect every phase of the problem of revelation and reason, including natural and international law, and the cultural enterprise as a whole. Any improper view has consequences the more drastic as its implications are applied to regenerate and to unregenerate man, from primal origin to final destiny.[3]

The capital punishment debate is no exception to this observation. Criminal or not, each individual bears God's image and must be treated accordingly, that is, with dignity and worth. Any penalty that degrades humans by treating them as if they had no worth is immoral. So we ask: Does capital punishment per se do this?

First of all, does capital punishment treat individuals as objects to be used for society's benefit without regard to the interests or rights of the criminal? On the contrary, those who would seek to "cure" and "heal" people without receiving their consent treat them as less than human.[4] On the other hand, to punish criminals because they "deserve" it is to respect them as morally responsible persons created in God's image who knew better and therefore have earned this punishment.

Second, while we acknowledge that some types of executions did (and do) treat people as less than human, the concept of capital punishment is not in conflict with mankind bearing the *imago Dei*. God himself ordained capital punishment in the Old Testament.

Capital punishment was established by the image-Giver to protect the dignity of the image-bearers. Willful elimination of the expression of God's image from one individual by another (premeditated murder) merited the penalty of execution, i.e., the elimination of the expression of God's image from the murderer. There was no conflict between capital punishment and the *imago Dei*. Indeed, the former depends upon the latter.

Bailey discusses the divine rationale behind this principle:

> Life originated by a special act of the Deity (by the power of the divine breath, as the ancient story in Gen. 2:7 put it). Consequently, humans were not free to terminate it, save under conditions specified by God. Even food animals must be brought to the sanctuary and slaughtered in a prescribed ritual whereby the blood is removed. Failure to do so results in "bloodguilt" (Lev. 17:4), a term which is elsewhere used for the murder of a human being (Exod. 22:2). How much more the offense, therefore, if human life ("created in the image of God," Gen. 1:26) is taken without proper sanction! One has acted arrogantly against a life-force that is an extension of God's own life-giving power. It is, to put it boldly, "an attack upon God." Even an animal that kills a human is to be destroyed (Exod. 21:28). A human who does so all the more forfeits any right to life (Gen. 9:1–7).[5]

The death penalty, at least for premeditated murder, does not operate in opposition to human dignity. Rather, it was established in respect of human dignity derived from the *imago Dei* within each human being. Capital punishment, then, is the ultimate compliment to the human dignity of both victim and murderer it implies the most pro-human stance possible. There are, of course, forms of capital punishment which violate human dignity and worth, but the concept is entirely compatible with God's standards of human worth. On the other hand, a penalty of ten years in prison for premeditated murder devalues human life by saying that the victim's life was worth only ten years of penalty. Equity and justice demand a punishment that matches the crime. Capital punishment for premeditated murder provides equity and justice as well as values human life.

Capital Punishment and the Sixth Commandment

When Moses descended from Mount Sinai, he gave Israel ten summary commandments which were to guide their personal lives as God's covenant people. The Sixth Commandment seems to rule out any form of capital punishment: "Thou shalt not kill" (Exod. 20:13).[6] Since capital punishment involves killing, it seems to be a *"prima facie* violation of this fundamental moral principle."* Yet, one chapter later God ordered the death penalty for intentional murder.

Has God become a transgressor of his law, or is there another concept at work? Obviously, the latter is the case, and we find that God has established two arenas of moral activity: private and public morality. What seems inconsistent at first glance becomes comprehensible when these two aspects of God's established order are taken into account. What is immoral in one arena—for example, killing a person—may be completely moral in another, e.g., the death penalty. This answers the problem raised by God's orders to Israel to engage in total warfare against the Canaanite tribes. Israel's armies were God's tools of judgment against the sinful rebellion of these people. It also answers the problem raised by the eschatological judgments in which the returning Christ will destroy his enemies in a fierce, destructive battle. Individuals acting as proper agents of governments can do things that are prohibited to them as private citizens. Scripture affirms both public and private moralities as distinct realms of activity.

We find that both Old and New Testaments recognize the existence of human governments. Romans 13:1–7 is the most general statement regarding government in the New Testament.

My neighbor would think it strange if I demanded that he pay me money so that I would personally police our neighborhood. But few people think it strange to pay taxes to governmental bodies to provide police service. Were my neighbor to refuse my demands and I were to lock him in my cellar for a year or two, I would be adjudged a public menace. Government, however, may imprison tax dodgers and in some cases risk public clamor if it refuses to do so. Clearly, governments can do things that individuals cannot, and this has been ordained by God.

When a person argues against capital punishment based on the Sixth Commandment he or she is ignoring the division between individual and governmental morality, between murder and prescribed killing. No person is permitted to murder or kill another. But God has established governmental authority and given it the responsibility for punishing crime—applying, if necessary, the death penalty. Personal vengeance, however, is not permitted:

> Do not take revenge, my friends, but leave room for God's wrath, for it is written: "It is mine to avenge I will repay," says the Lord. (Rom. 12:19, citing Deuteronomy 32:35 NIV)

Vengeance is God's, and government is one method whereby he exercises this vengeance. Punishment is the responsibility of government, not individuals. Capital punishment is not a violation of God's moral code. Perhaps no biblical reference illustrates the difference between personal and public morality in the realm of capital punishment better than Deuteronomy 21:18–21:

> If a man has a stubborn and rebellious son who does not obey his father and mother and will not listen to them when they discipline him, his father and mother shall take hold of him and bring him to the elders at the gate of his town. They shall say to the elders, "This son of ours is stubborn and rebellious. He will not obey us. He is a profligate and a drunkard." Then all the men of his town shall stone him to death. You must purge the evil from among you. All Israel will hear of it and be afraid.

If the parents had executed their son before they brought him to the government officials (the elders at the gate), they would have been guilty of murder and been punished by those same elders. However, when they present their rebellious son to the elders for official condemnation, the situation changes. Their word becomes the basis of the capital charge and the father becomes one of the executioners (the men of his town). He now acts as an agent of the government and may carry out an act which was forbidden to him as a private citizen. Acts of personal vengeance are condemned as murder, but acts of capital punishment, being sanctioned by the government, are proper. We do not argue that juvenile delinquents should be executed, but we use this reference to establish once and for all that a distinction exists between private and public morality.

Capital Punishment and Inequitable Application

We acknowledge that major inequities exist in the application of capital punishment today. Many have pointed to these as justification for the abolition of the death penalty lest it be applied unfairly. All these arguments, however, raise the same issue: problems in the *application* of capital punishment, not the *concept* of capital punishment. Our discussion concerns the defense of the death penalty as a valid punishment that may be dispensed by government, not necessarily the defense of our current system in its application at every point. However, we will consider these arguments in some detail, for at first glance they do seem persuasive.

Many have recognized the disproportionate number of disadvantaged criminals on death rows. One of these critics, Byron Eshelman, writing in *Death Row Chaplain*, claims that

> as it is now applied, the death penalty is nothing but an arbitrary discrimination against an occasional victim. It cannot even be said that it is reserved as a weapon of retributive justice for the most atrocious criminals. For it is not necessarily the most guilty who suffer it. Almost any criminal with wealth or influence can escape it, but the poor and friendless convict, without means to fight his case from court to court or to exert pressure upon the pardoning executive, is the one singled out as a sacrifice to what is little more than a tradition.[7]

Race is also said to be a factor in discriminatory application of the death penalty. For example, a study by an Iowa law professor found that

76

in Georgia, blacks were 4.3 times as likely to receive the death penalty for killing whites than whites were for killing blacks.[8] Assuming the accuracy of these statistics, capital punishment may be applied unfairly. But this does not justify eliminating the death penalty as a morally proper punishment.

The same line of reasoning, we argue, could be employed to eliminate all other legal penalties. Politicians "fix" parking tickets, influential doctors avoid conviction on malpractice suits, and the rich employ skillful lawyers who get convictions overturned on technicalities. Shall we then do away with all forms of punishment because of inequities, or shall we seek to reform our judicial systems to eliminate such practices? The answer is obvious. We must distinguish between the moral question and the problem of discrimination. Ernest van den Haag speaks to the issue when he writes:

> Discrimination is irrelevant to this moral question. If the death penalty were distributed equally and uncapriciously and with super-human perfection to all the guilty, but were morally unjust, it would be unjust in each case. Contrariwise, if the death penalty is morally just, however discriminatorily applied to only some of the guilty, it remains just in each case in which it is applied.[9]

Capital Punishment and the Execution of the Innocent

A practical problem more serious than discrimination is the execution of innocent people. This is not a new problem. Indeed, it was anticipated in the Old Testament theocracy in which God established a detailed procedure for carrying out the death penalty:

1. The standard of proof required for conviction amounted to certainty,

2. conviction required the testimony of at least two witnesses,

3. the penalty for perjury in a capital case was execution; thus the witnesses were motivated to speak the truth,

4. in difficult cases the verdict was deferred to experts, reducing the problem of local prejudice, and

5. once the verdict was returned, it was unchangeable, thus motivating the courts to be accurate.

Our present criminal justice system would do well to model itself after these standards, for its deficiencies are obvious to all who take the time to look. However, failure to properly apply capital punishment does not make it immoral. Again, we note that the same argument could be made against most other forms of punishment. The courts can release an individual who has been imprisoned for a crime he or she did not commit, but it cannot return the lost time. Money can be returned, but lost time, reputations, careers, etc., cannot be restored. This should motivate us to ensure that only the guilty are punished, not to eliminate penalties for all crimes.

Summary

It is our conclusion that capital punishment is not contradictory to God's moral standards as revealed in either the Old or New Testaments. Humans bear the image of the eternal God and are to be accorded all the dignity and respect that the *imago Dei* requires. Applying the death penalty as retributive punishment, especially for premeditated murder, respects the dignity of both victim and murderer. The criminal has deliberately eliminated a personal expression of God's image and therefore is required to pay a suitable penalty: the elimination of the embodiment of God's image in and through him. Neither does the death penalty violate God's moral standard as expressed in the Decalogue. Personal vengeance is prohibited and capital punishment is given to governments to apply after proper investigations. Inequities in the application of the death penalty exist, but they are reasons for revamping our criminal justice system, not eliminating capital punishment. If the death penalty is eliminated because of such inequities, then all punishments should have to be eliminated because few, if any, are fairly applied. We find nothing in the commonly advanced moral arguments that requires the elimination of the death penalty as a proper, morally acceptable retribution for capital crimes.

NOTES

1. Ramsey Clark, cited by Georald H. Gottlied, "Capital Punishment," *Crime and Delinquency* 15 (January, 1970): 2–11.

2. *Furman* v. *Georgia*, 408 U.W. 238 (1972), cited by Walter Berns, *For Capital Punishment*, p. 27; see bibliography.

3. Carl F. H. Henry, "Image of God," *Evangelical Dictionary of Theology* (Grand Rapids, Mich.: Baker Book House, 1984), 546.

4. C. S. Lewis, *God in the Dock*, 292; see bibliography.

5. Lloyd R. Bailey, *Capital Punishment: What the Bible Says*, 34–35; see bibliography.

6. The verb translated "kill" in the KJV occurs almost fifty times in the Old Testament as in every relevant use means "to murder," especially with premeditation involved. The LXX translates it with the Greek word for "murder." Consequently the NIV's translation is the more accurate: "You shall not murder."

7. Byron E. Eshelman, *Death Row Chaplain* (Englewood Cliffs, N.J.: Prentice Hall, 1962), 223.

8. Anthony Parker, "Death Penalty Opponents Weigh Change in Strategy," *Sojourners* (June 1988): 12.

9. Ernest van den Haag, "In Defense of the Death Penalty: A Practical and Moral Analysis," *The Death Penalty in America* (New York: Plenum Press, 1983).

6

Does Capital Punishment
Deter Murderers?

Does capital punishment deter crime, specifically premeditated murder? This issue has long been the rallying cry for both supporters and opponents of the death penalty. Its supporters claim that capital punishment is a deterrent and therefore should be retained. Opponents, on the other hand, claim that capital punishment does not deter murder and consequently should be abolished. Both camps have done studies and counter-studies and each has concluded its view is correct.

Other issues, however, are more basic to the question of capital punishment than deterrence, and we have already discussed a number of these in previous chapters. Justification of the death penalty, especially for premeditated murder, rests on foundational issues of theology and philosophy and these, as we have shown, permit the state to apply the death penalty for premeditated murder. Since the primary purpose of capital punishment is retribution, the death penalty is morally justified apart from practical issues such as deterrence. However, this secondary issue needs to be addressed. If capital punishment is a divinely established moral imperative for the state, then its proper application should produce observable results. This issue, then is the subject of this chapter.

THE DEATH PENALTY DEBATE

Deterrence Defined

To deter is "to turn aside, discourage, or prevent from acting by fear or consideration of dangerous, difficult, or unpleasant attendant circumstances or consequences." Capital punishment, something normally considered "difficult" and "unpleasant," should discourage individuals from committing murder.[1]

Ernest van den Haag, a supporter of capital punishment, defines deterrence as "a preconscious, general response to a severe but not necessarily specifically and explicitly apprehended or calculated threat."[2] Hugo Adam Bedau, an opponent of the death penalty, criticizes van den Haag's definition as too vague and general, and suggests a more explicit definition.

> A given punishment (P) is a deterrent for a given person (A) with respect to a given crime (C) at a given time (t) if and only if A does not commit C at t because he runs the risk of P if he commits C, and A prefers, *ceteris paribus*, not to suffer P for committing C.[3]

C. H. S. Jayewardene, another opponent of capital punishment, defines deterrence as comprising two components:

> The prevention of the commission of a crime by those who have already committed it once and the prevention of the commission of a crime by those who have not committed it before.[4]

He also gives another, simpler, definition: "more without, less with."[5]

The question, then, is whether the death penalty helps deter crime. Does the potential for execution dissuade potential criminals, notably those bent on premeditated murder, from committing the crime? The question, for some, is not secondary. Some have argued that this is the only possible justification for any criminal penalty. This view gained wide popularity through the 1764 work of Cesare Beccaria *On Crimes and Punishments*. He argued that punishment "should consist of only such gradations of intensity as suffice to deter men from committing crimes."[6] Based on this principle, Beccaria argued that a life sentence would be a greater deterrent than an execution, since the example would last longer.

This view was adopted and adapted by many others, including English jurist and philosopher Jeremy Bentham. His dictum is still held today:

> The end of law is to augment happiness. The general object which all laws have, or ought to have, in common, is to augment the total happiness of the community, and therefore, in the first place to exclude, as far as may be, everything that tends to subtract from that happiness: in other words to exclude mischief.... General prevention ought to be the chief end of punishment as it is its real justification.[7]

We, however, argue that deterrence of crime does not justify the death penalty or any other punishment as part of a society's criminal justice system. Punishment is designed by God to be a just retribution for criminal acts. Since mankind bears the image of the Creator, and since retribution is the Creator's revealed purpose for punishment, we would expect that such punishment, properly administered, would be a deterrent. That being the case, we will first examine the deterrent effect of punishment in general.

The Theory of Deterrence

Deterrence, even in theory, can never be offered as the final justification for punishment of any kind. If this were the case, there would be no theoretical limit to the punishment applied, nor any limit as to who received it. A convicted person, for example, could receive as much or as little punishment as the judge felt necessary to provide an adequate deterrent for the rest of society. Indeed, the same crime might be given vastly differing penalties if the only motive were deterrence. Furthermore, if deterrence is the only justification for punishment, then there is no essential requirement that the person punished be guilty. A teacher could, for example, punish an innocent student to give the class an example of what would happen if a certain rule is broken.[8] Such action, however, would be a serious injustice rather than a proper deterrent. True justice requires a direct connection between the crime committed and the penalty assessed. Deterrence as the sole justification for punishment does not provide that essential link. However, it can be a result of proper punishment.

Is punishment intended to have a deterrent effect? The biblical answer is yes. While deterrence is not the justification for punishment within God's established order, it is one result. This is clear in both the Old and New Testaments. Under Israel's theocracy Yahweh expected that punishment, including capital punishment, would deter his people from committing crimes.

> The man who shows contempt for the judge or for the priest who stands ministering there to the LORD your God must be put to death. You must purge the evil from Israel. All the people will hear and be afraid, and will not be contemptuous again. (Deut. 17:12–13 NIV)

In the case of a disputed testimony in court,

> The judges must make a thorough investigation, and if the witness proves to be a liar, giving false testimony against his brother, then do to him as he intended to do to his brother. You must purge the evil from among you. The rest of the people will hear of this and be afraid, and never again will such an evil thing be done among you. Show no pity: life for life, eye for eye, tooth for tooth, hand for hand, foot for foot. (Deut. 19:18–21 NIV)

The same concept is also found in Deuteronomy 21:18–21, again involving capital punishment.

The same connection between punishment and deterrence is also found in the New Testament: "Those [elders] who sin are to be rebuked publicly, so that the others may take warning" (1 Tim. 5:20 NIV). Likewise, Peter told his readers that Sodom and Gomorrah were made examples "of what is going to happen to the ungodly" (2 Pet. 2:6 NIV). God expects deterrence to be one result of the proper application of punishment. What, then, constitutes "proper application" of punishment?

A proper application of punishment must be timely and just. For the penalty to deter crime effectively, the population at large must recognize that wrongs are quickly punished. The longer the wait between the act and the retribution the less clear the connection of the two. Also, the punishment must be just. Cruel retribution or excessive leniency only confuse justice and do not aid deterrence.

Does Capital Punishment Deter Murderers?

Current studies on the type of punishment that best deters crime are inconclusive. Some have led investigators to conclude that no punishment is an effective deterrent. Other studies show that lenient penalties (such as fines, probation, suspended sentences) are equally as effective as more severe punishments in deterring crime. There is, however, no consensus on the matter.[9] Likewise, there is no consensus on the deterrent effect of capital punishment as currently administered in our society.

Empirical Studies of Deterrence

A common argument against capital punishment is its lack of deterrent value. Many would agree with the *Christian Century* essayist who rejected the death penalty on this basis:

The five states with fewest murders relative to populations are all states which have for many years made no legal provision for the death penalty. The Canadian Parliament voted out the last remnants of capital punishment for murder several years ago, and Canada has about one-fourth the rate of murders the U.S. has. Japan and most countries of Western Europe have no death penalty in the civilian penal code, and their rates of criminal homicide run from one-eighth to one-seventeenth of ours. Speed and high probability of arrest and punishment have a significant effect. Severity has little deterrent effect and is often counter-productive.[10]

Many have tried to establish statistical evidence for or against the deterrent effect of capital punishment, but no one has produced unambiguous results. There is almost uniform agreement that no study has provided clear statistical "proof" about the deterrent effect of capital punishment one way or another. In 1976, for example, the United States Supreme Court concluded that:

Statistical attempts to evaluate the worth of the death penalty as a deterrent to crimes by potential offenders have occasioned a great deal of debate. The results simply have been inconclusive. (*Gregg v. Georgia*, 1976)[11]

In 1978 the National Academy of Sciences published a report by its Panel on Research on Deterrent and Incapacitative Effects. The panel concluded "that the available studies provide no useful evidence on the deterrent effect of capital punishment."[12] The report also stated that the complex nature of the subject and the lack of scientifically acceptable evidence made such research difficult at best. It concluded that "Research on the deterrent effects of capital sanctions is not likely to provide results that will or *should have* much influence on policy makers" (emphasis added).[13]

Walter Berns, writing in support of capital punishment, identifies several basic problems which confront all statistical studies of this nature.[14] (1) The problem of identifying the single effect of the threat of capital punishment among the many factors which affect the decision to commit murder, (2) the impossibility of measuring the number of potential murderers that the death penalty deterred from committing the crime, and, (3) over the past ten years the number of executions in the United States has been so low that any deterrent of capital punishment has been eliminated since it is not a practical threat.

In spite of these difficulties, researchers have tried to statistically investigate the deterrent effect of capital punishment. One such study was published in 1959 by Thorsten Sellin.[15] Sellin's study involved comparing the homicide rates in contiguous states, some with and some without the death penalty. He assumed that these states were, as much as possible, similar in character of population, social and economic conditions. He also looked for correlations between the homicide rates and the legal status of the death penalty. Additionally, he studied the murder rate within a state that has abolished the death penalty and then reimposed it. His conclusion was that the death penalty has no effect on the murder rate. His work, however, was flawed by the problems Berns identified. Among the specific problems of Sellin's work was his assumption that the states investigated were completely equal. But regardless of how equal two states appear to be, there is no way to know that they are equal without careful analysis. Such variables as criminal apprehension, ease of convictions, and ideas of racial prejudice are all factors which can change the results in a study, variables that Sellin did not consider.

The fact that Sellin correlated the homicide rate with the legal status of the death penalty rather than the number of executions actually carried out is another major flaw in his work. The simple threat of any punishment will never deter as much as the punishment enforced. Although the death penalty was in effect for fifty years, if there were only five executions of three hundred and fifty death row inmates in the last twenty years, the deterrent factor could not possibly be measured accurately.

In 1975 Isaac Ehrlich published another study based on a completely different approach.[16] As an econometrician, Ehrlich applied the mathematics of economics to the study of capital punishment. His purpose was to take into consideration some of the variables left untouched by the previous types of studies. Ehrlich employed

> multiple regression analysis to investigate the possible relationships between one of a number of possible "causes" or independent variables, and a particular "effect" or dependent variable. He constructed a mathematical model of a "murder supply function" and treated its elements as [one would] treat inflation, the bank discount rate, or increases in the rate of the money supply.[17]

Ehrlich assumed in his study that some murderers expect to gain more from murdering than from not murdering and who calculate the probable losses and gains of their action. His conclusions were

> on the average the trade-off between the execution of an offender and the lives of potential victims it might have saved was of the order of magnitude of 1 for 8 for the period 1933–67 in the United States. . . . Each execution may deter as many as eight murders.[18]

This conclusion resulted from utilizing variables such as the most likely age-group to commit murder, unemployment rate, labor force participation rate, and per capita income. As well, it is possible that the number of murders may have diminished systematically over time due to improvement in medical technology.

Despite the monumental effort to account for a multitude of variables and attitudes not calculated in the previous studies, critics have leveled serious charges against this study. Moreover, they have also conducted similar studies by similar means but have arrived at opposing results. Sociologists such as Hans Zeisel, Laurence Klein, Victor Filatov, and William C. Bailey have attempted similar studies analyzing still other variables and have received results opposing Ehrlich's.[19] All of this simply reinforces the above-quoted opinions, that such studies will never yield unambiguous results.

Even though the statistical evidence supporting the deterrent effect of capital punishment is inconclusive, there is anecdotal evidence that the death penalty does deter potential murderers. Many murders are committed in a burst of passion, but premeditated murder requires rational thought and choices. The potential of execution must enter into consideration in these cases. After all, fear of death has deterred thousands of people from flying, smoking, overeating, etc. It is only reasonable to suppose that potential murderers would be deterred by the possibility of execution. The testimony of law-enforcement personnel supports this conclusion. The sheriff of Los Angeles County testified before the California Senate Committee on the Judiciary that "the overwhelming majority of people in law enforcement—the ones who are dealing with these criminals, the ones who are seeing them not as statistics but real live human beings, and who are studying their human behavior—are overwhelmingly convinced that capital punishment is a deterrent."[20]

The district attorney of Philadelphia added to this when he testified before the United States Senate: "We have the frequent occurrence in the criminal courts of Philadelphia where professional burglars have expressed themselves on the point of not carrying a weapon on a burglary because of their concern there may be a scuffle, there may be a dispute, the weapon may be used and death result and . . . they may face the possibility of capital punishment."[21] Other anecdotes could be added, but our point has been made.

Summary

Support of capital punishment does not ultimately rest on its deterrent effect, but its retributive role, especially for premeditated murder. If the death penalty has failed to deter murder, and we are not convinced that this is the case, then this apparent failing must be measured against the lack of swift, consistent application of capital punishment. The failure—if, indeed, there is a failure—is in the administration and application of, rather than the theory of, capital punishment.

NOTES

1. Our discussion will center on premeditated murder without evaluating the application of the death penalty to those convicted of other crimes.

2. Vincent E. Barry, *Applying Ethics, A Text with Readings* (Belmont, Calif.: Wadsworth Publishing Co., 1985), 268.

3. Ibid., 268.

4. C. H. S. Jayewardene, *The Penalty of Death* (Lexington, Mass.: Lexington Books, 1977), 10–11.

5. Ibid., 9.

6. Cesare Beccaria, *On Crimes and Punishments*, 47–48; see bibliography.

7. Charles F. Abel and Frank H. Marsh, *Punishment and Restitution*, 70; see bibliography.

8. C. S. Lewis, *God in the Dock*, 291; see the bibliography.

9. See Hugo Bedau, *The Death Penalty in America*, 277; see bibliography. See also Alfred Blumstein, Jacqueline Cohen, and Daniel Nagin, eds. *Deterrence and Incapacitation: Estimating the Effects of Criminal Sanctions on Crime Rates* (Washington D.C.: National Academy of Sciences, 1978), 9.

10. L. Harold, "The Death Penalty: Not a Remedy but a Symptom," *The Christian Century* (January 30, 1980): 93.

11. "The Capital Punishment Debate," The Standing Committee for Church in Society, American Lutheran Church, 1985, 3.

12. Alfred Blumstein, et. al, *Deterrence and Incapacitation*, 9.

13. Ibid.

14. Walter Berns, *For Capital Punishment*, 87–92; see bibliography.

15. Thorsten Sellin, *The Death Penalty: A Report for the Modern Penal Code Project of the American Law Institute* (Philadelphia: American Law Institute, 1959).

16. Isaac Ehrlich, "The Deterrent Effect of Capital Punishment: A Question of Life and Death," *American Economic Review* 65 (June 1975).

17. Walter Berns, *For Capital Punishment*, 98.

18. Ehrlich, 398.

19. Bedau, *The Death Penalty in America*, 96–97.

20. California Legislature, Senate Committee on the Judiciary, p. 150 (1969), cited in "The Capital Punishment Debate," Standing Committee for Church in Society, American Lutheran Church, 1985, 5.

21. Ibid.

7

Is Capital Punishment Constitutional?

The Eighth Amendment to the Constitution of the United States reads: "Excessive bail shall not be required, nor excessive fines imposed, nor cruel and unusual punishments inflicted." Recent judicial debate has focused on whether capital punishment is to be considered "cruel and unusual" punishment. There are those who argue that capital punishment for any reason is ruled out by this limitation. Supporters of capital punishment note that the framers of the Constitution did not prohibit executions for capital crimes when they spoke against cruel and unusual punishments. At the heart of the issue is the constitutional meaning of "cruel and unusual" and how these terms apply to capital punishment. This chapter will evaluate the arguments relating to the constitutionality of capital punishment.

Important Judicial Decisions

In the 1970s there were two major decisions by the United States Supreme Court regarding capital punishment which helped clarify the contemporary understanding of capital punishment and the issue of "cruel and unusual" punishment—*Furman* v. *Georgia* (1972) and *Gregg* v. *Georgia* (1976). Though Furman challenged the constitutionality of the death penalty's application, Gregg and a quartet of cases decided the same day as Gregg—*Proffitt* v. *Florida, Jurek* v. *Texas, Woodson* v. *North Carolina,* and *Roberts* v. *Louisiana*—rejected the argument that imposing the death penalty

91

under any circumstances constitutes cruel and unusual punishment in violation of the Eighth and Fourteenth Amendments.[1]

Furman v. *Georgia.* Prior to 1971 the United States judicial system allowed juries to determine the penalty in a first degree (premeditated) murder case. Once the jury found a defendant guilty of first degree murder, it proceeded to decide the penalty. Usually this decision was part of the initial deliberation and was made without any additional evidence or guidance from the legislature or the Court.[2] In 1971 the United States Supreme Court began to consider constitutional challenges to this system. Initially, in *McGaut* v. *California* (1971) the Court voted 5–3 to uphold the constitutionality of the state's death penalty statutes which permitted this procedure.[3]

In 1972, however, the Court reviewed these same state statutes in *Furman* v. *Georgia.* In a 5–4 vote they determined that such procedures were unconstitutional. The five justices in the majority wrote five separate opinions presenting different reasons for their decisions. The one concept common to all of their opinions was that the death penalty was arbitrarily applied.[4]

Chief Justice Warren Burger dissented and spoke of the "uncertain language" of the Eighth Amendment.[5] But Justice William Brennan, siding with the majority, argued that without the Eighth Amendment's prohibition of cruel and unusual punishments, "the legislature would otherwise have had the unfiltered power to prescribe punishments for crimes."[6] He also added that if the legislature is to be restrained, the judiciary must be willing to enforce its prohibition. The "cruel and unusual" clause, Justice Brennan argued, must draw its meaning from the "evolving standards of decency that mark the progress of a maturing society."[7] According to Brennan,[8] the Court should use four principles when deciding whether a punishment is prohibited by the "cruel and unusual punishment clause":

1. A punishment must not be so severe as to be degrading to human dignity;

2. The state must not arbitrarily inflict a severe punishment;

3. A severe punishment must not be unacceptable to contemporary society;

4. A severe punishment must not be excessive.[9]

In Justice Brennan's mind capital punishment qualified as cruel and unusual punishment on all four counts.

Justice Thurgood Marshall was the other majority voice in Furman who argued that capital punishment under all circumstances was cruel and unusual. He also believed that the death penalty was not in accord with the "evolving standard of decency" of contemporary society. His opinion presented four principles to determine whether or not a punishment is cruel and unusual:

1. Punishments that amount to torture are prohibited;

2. Punishments that were previously unknown as penalties for a given offense may be unconstitutional;

3. A penalty may be cruel and unusual because it is excessive and serves no valid legislative purpose;

4. A penalty may be cruel and unusual because it is abhorrent to currently existing moral values.[10]

Justice Marshall's argument rested on the second two principles. In his own words, "capital punishment serves no purpose that life imprisonment could not serve equally well" and therefore "there is no basis for concluding that capital punishment is not excessive." Furthermore, "even if capital punishment is not excessive, it nonetheless violates the Eighth Amendment because it is morally unacceptable to the people of the United States at this time in their history."[11]

Justices William Douglas, Potter Stewart, and Byron White, the other majority justices in Furman, did not carry their arguments as far as Marshall and Brennan. Their arguments focused on the defects in the justice system's sentencing practices. These defects, they claimed, violated the Eighth Amendment rather than the death penalty itself.[12]

Those who felt that *Furman* v. *Georgia* would put an end to capital punishment were disappointed because the decision left some major questions unanswered. Justice Harry Blackmun, who strongly opposed capital punishment, nonetheless wrote a dissenting opinion in Furman which raised some crucial questions regarding the majority opinion. He cited numerous cases from 1879–1963 in which the Supreme Court was either implicitly or explicitly unanimous in that "capital punishment was . . . not unconstitutional per se under the Eighth Amendment."[13] Justice Blackmun asked three crucial questions:

1. Why should the death penalty be regarded as cruel and unusual punishment?

2. What evidence is there to support the claim that the "passage of time" has produced the relevant kind of evolutionary development in standards of decency in the United States from which the Eighth Amendment "must draw its meaning"?

3. Why is now (1972) the time to strike down the death penalty?[14]

Furthermore, Blackmun argued that it was the legislative, not the judicial, branch of the government that was far more in tune with the moral climate of the nation and that legislators are the proper actors to bring about the abolishment of the death penalty. Because these questions were not properly addressed in the Furman decision, the door was left open for further Supreme Court review of the issue.

Gregg v. *Georgia.* After Furman, states which desired to exercise capital punishment established judicial standards to help juries exercise proper discretion in deciding between death and life as a penalty. These states also instituted new jury procedures to eliminate the arbitrariness in their death penalty systems.[15] Essentially, these new standards required the jury to find that a first-degree murder case is also characterized by one of a fixed list of aggravating circumstances before a defendant can be sentenced to death. Greater scrutiny was also required in analyzing mitigating circumstances relating to the appropriateness of the death sentence in the case. These states also established a two-stage trial procedure. The first trial would determine guilt or innocence and then, if the verdict is guilty of first degree murder, a separate trial would decide the appropriate penalty.[16]

In spite of the changes brought by Furman, there was strong public support for the death penalty. On July 2, 1976, the Supreme Court issued their ruling on *Gregg* v. *Georgia.* The petitioners in Gregg argued, as in Furman, that standards of decency had evolved to the point where capital punishment could no longer be tolerated. They argued that in view of the evolution of standards of decency, the Eighth Amendment should be interpreted as prohibiting capital punishment.

The Gregg Court agreed that "contemporary values" were relevant in determining the constitutionality of the issue and set out to look for objective measures of those values. The Court concluded that capital punishment was constitutionally valid and not in violation of the "cruel and unusual punishment" clause.

The Court concluded that developments during the four years since Furman have undercut substantially the assumptions upon which Furman's arguments rested. . . . It is now evident that a large proportion of American society continues to regard it as an appropriate and necessary criminal sanction.[17]

The most marked indication of society's endorsement of the death penalty for murder was the legislative response to Furman. Legislatures of at least thirty-five states enacted new statutes that provide for the death penalty for at least some crimes which result in the death of another person.[18]

The Court went on to cite the State of California's constitutional amendment authorizing capital punishment after the Supreme Court in *California* v. *People of Anderson* ruled against California's death penalty statutes. The Court further noted that juries across the United States reflected a general support for capital punishment. Thus, because of public opinion and legislative response to Furman, the Court ruled in Gregg that the "evolving standards of decency" argument favored the support of capital punishment. They, therefore, affirmed its constitutionality.

In retrospect, the Supreme Court ruled on Gregg so soon after their ruling in Furman because of the change brought by Furman. In response to *Furman* v. *Georgia* many states passed new laws governing the death penalty process, laws that met the tests of Furman. Although the Court had not outlawed the death penalty in its Furman decision, it had raised questions about what kind of capital punishment system, if any, the Court might approve.[19] Now the Court had to decide the constitutionality of the new procedures.[20] This was the context in which the Court ruled on Gregg. In other cases, namely *Proffitt* v. *Florida, Jurek* v. *Texas, Woodson* v. *North Carolina,* and *Roberts* v. *Louisiana,* the Court affirmed the constitutionality of capital punishment. But not everyone was convinced.

Arguments Favoring Capital Punishment as Constitutional

Ernest van den Haag defended the constitutionality of capital punishment in a debate with John P. Conrad. First of all, van den Haag appealed to the Fifth Amendment and its due process clause. The Fifth

Amendment reads, in part, that "(no one shall) be deprived of life, liberty or property, without due process of law . . . ." Van den Haag reasoned that "The Fifth Amendment implies that with 'due process of law' one may be deprived of 'life, liberty or property' (i.e., that the death penalty is a legitimate punishment)."[21] Furthermore, he argued,

> Since the prohibition of "cruel and unusual punishment" was enacted at the same time, obviously it was not meant to repeal the death penalty, which at the time was imposed frequently.[22]

Another argument offered by van den Haag involved his philosophy of constitutional interpretation. He sided with those who believe the basic issue in constitutional interpretation is the intent of the framers. Consequently, he posed the question:

> Is what we consider "cruel and unusual" today to determine whether laws imposing the death penalty are constitutional or should we be guided by what the framers of the Constitution meant by cruel and unusual?[23]

According to van den Haag, if we are bound by what the framers intended, then that constitutional interpretation is binding until the document is amended. Consequently, in view of the Fifth Amendment, the death penalty must be seen to be constitutional. He asked, "If we are to be guided by what we want and not by what the framers of the Constitution decided, why have a Constitution?"[24] This strikes at the heart of the "evolving standard of decency" criteria argued by Justices Brennan and Marshall in Furman.

Even allowing for the "evolving standards of decency" argument, van den Haag noted that the majority of Americans (in 1983) favored capital punishment. He cited polls showing that 70 percent of the populace favor the death penalty. He also stressed what the Supreme Court had recognized in Gregg:

> When the Supreme Court objected to some aspect of state laws imposing capital punishment, more than two-thirds of all the states reenacted them so as to remove putative constitutional defects.[25]

Van den Haag, however, did not believe that constitutional interpretation should be subject to public opinion. He argued that public opinion is best dealt with through the legislative branch of government, not the judiciary.

He further defended capital punishment on the basis of a careful analysis of the Eighth Amendment itself. He reasoned that the Eighth Amendment "prohibits cruel and unusual punishment, not cruel *or* unusual punishment." Therefore, a punishment must be cruel *and* unusual to be unconstitutional.[26]

Thus, according to this view, the framers meant to outlaw unusual punishment, if cruel, but not cruel punishment, if usual.[27] A punishment would have to be different (unusual) and cruel, both, to be unconstitutional. Van den Haag did not see the death penalty as "unusual" in the Eighth Amendment sense.

In determining whether the death penalty should at least be considered cruel, van den Haag discussed the two possible legal meanings of "cruel." First of all, "cruel may mean disproportionate, either to the seriousness of the crime or to other penalties (i.e., death penalty for thieves or pickpockets)."[28] Secondly, "cruel" could involve the infliction of gratuitous pain, pain not intended likely to achieve a rational end that may justify it (i.e., killing an animal for food vs. torturing an animal for fun).[29] With regards to the first legal aspect of "cruel," the death penalty hardly seems excessive when it is a punishment for murder. Van den Haag then argues, regarding the second aspect of "cruel," that while the death penalty is the most unpleasant of all punishments, it does at least have a rational basis. He claimed that

> it has rational purposes: to signify that murder is the worst and therefore the most severely punished crime; to indicate that murder is different from other crimes punished by prison; to show that there is a discontinuity signified by a different discontinuous punishment; and, not least, to deter others committing murder.[30]

Since the death penalty is not excessive as a punishment for murder and since it does have a rational basis for it, van den Haag concludes that it cannot be considered "cruel" and certainly not "unusual."

Conclusion

In assessing these arguments concerning the constitutionality of capital punishment, it is apparent that the root of the difference is the philosophical question: How do we interpret the Constitution? If, as Conrad (van den Haag's opponent) and certain Supreme Court justices reason, that those who sit on the bench ultimately decide what the Constitution means in contemporary society, then the document is practically worthless. A document has certain intrinsic meaning or it doesn't. If Supreme Court justices can read their own meanings into the Constitution then they are actually above the Constitution in terms of their authority rather than being bound to it by oath.

If, on the other hand, the Supreme Court is to take the Constitution's basic, original meaning and apply it to today's society, the justices should try to understand what the framers intended to say in the document. On this issue even Conrad admits that the "cruel and unusual" punishment clause of the Eighth Amendment was not intended by the framers to restrict capital punishment.

Van den Haag makes a good argument that, on the basis of the Fifth Amendment and on colonial practices, the framers did see times when capital punishment is not cruel since, for murder, the punishment fits the crime and there is a strong rationale for it. Conrad sees capital punishment as cruel and unusual on the basis of an "evolving standard of decency." This opinion is purely subjective and is not even consistent with current public opinion. In conclusion, those that argue in favor of capital punishment seem to be on strong constitutional ground.

NOTES

1. Franklin E. Zimring and Gordon Hawkins, *Capital Punishment and the American Agenda*, 50; see bibliography.
2. Barry Nakell and Kenneth A. Hardy. *The Arbitrariness of the Death Penalty* (Philadelphia: Temple University Press, 1987), 9.
3. Ibid.
4. Ibid.
5. Zimring and Hawkins, 51.
6. Ibid., 63.
7. Ibid., 53.

8. I have spoken of Brennan's perspective of the death penalty elsewhere: "[Brennan] considers capital punishment to be in violation of the Eighth Amendment against cruel and unusual punishment. This very statement portends that he can understand the meaning of the Eighth Amendment [elsewhere he indicates that we cannot understand the intent of the Framers]. But he contends that modern society has raised itself above the eighteenth century's archaic morality which advocated the death penalty. This position, however, is wrought with inconsistency since the Eighth Amendment is in tandem with the provisions for capital crimes. Moreover, the morality of the eighteenth century in this area has not significantly fluctuated to the present day. Consistently, the public has favored capital punishment by large margins.

So how does Brennan support this thesis? He substitutes *his* wisdom for that of the Framers who included capital punishment, those Justices who have not sequaciously followed him, and the public, he admits, who in general disagree with him. This assuredly is problematic for a Justice who has sworn to uphold and defend the Constitution and is required to serve under good behavior." H. Wayne House, ed., *Restoring the Constitution* (Dallas: Probe Books, 1987), 5.

9. Ibid.
10. Ibid., 54–55.
11. Ibid., 55.
12. Ibid., 56.
13. Ibid., 52.
14. Ibid.
15. Nakell and Hardy, 9.
16. Ibid.
17. Ibid., 65.
18. Zimring and Hawkins, 65.
19. Nakell and Hardy, 28.
20. Ibid.
21. Ernest van den Haag and John P. Conrad, *The Death Penalty: A Debate*, 157; see bibliography.
22. Ibid., 157.
23. Ibid., 158.
24. Ibid. See the article by Jeffrey A. Aman and H. Wayne House, "Constitutional Intrepretation and the Question of Lawful Authority," *Restoring the Constitution*, 191–211.
25. Ibid.
26. Ibid., 203.
27. Ibid.
28. Ibid.
29. Ibid., 204.
30. Ibid.

8

Reaffirming the Death Penalty for Today

We began our study by evaluating the various motives behind punishment to determine what reason best corresponds with the biblical data. Criminologists have suggested several different reasons for punishment, including rehabilitation, protection of society, and retribution. The last reason, retribution, probably is the least favored today and, certainly, is the least understood. Most equate it with personal vengeance or a ritual catharsis of society's collective guilt. Retribution, however, simply means that every act merits a previously determined recompense. Wages, for example, may be considered positive retribution in that they are usually agreed to before the work is done and, when the job or number of hours is successfully completed, the worker is given his or her just due. Retributive punishment works the same way: society identifies undesirable acts which it deems harmful and agrees upon penalties for these acts. When a person commits one of these acts, he or she receives the penalty due that act.

Retribution is the basic reason presented by Scripture for punishment in a criminal justice system. The Noachian Covenant identified execution as the penalty for premeditated murder. The more detailed Mosaic Code identified numerous proscribed acts for Israel and allocated various penalties for those acts. This legal system identified almost twenty actions as capital crimes, including premeditated murder. The individual Israelite knew beforehand what the prohibited acts were and what penalties he or she would suffer if any were committed. God's Word teaches retributive punishment.

Unlike other concepts, such as rehabilitation, retribution provides limits on punishment. Each act merits a given penalty, no more and no less. If the motivation is only to rehabilitate the criminal, then there are no theoretical limits to the punishment. He may be given "whatever it takes" to achieve the desired end. Retributional limits, "eye for eye, tooth for tooth," restrict punishment to the prescribed penalty for a given act. Criminals know in advance what they will suffer and have the protection of law, even in their punishment.

Retribution respects the dignity of the criminal. If the purpose of punishment is to protect society from crime, then the criminal becomes nothing more than an object lesson and may suffer whatever is necessary to convey the lesson to his culture. In fact, there is no essential requirement that the one punished be guilty. If the group will learn its lesson by watching punishment in action, then there is no philosophical reason why the one punished has to be guilty. Perhaps the lesson could be taught by punishing one of the group's weaker members, even though he or she is innocent. Retribution, on the other hand, recognizes the inherent dignity of the individual by making him or her responsible for his choice. The criminal chose to act; therefore, he or she will receive the consequence of that action. Retribution acknowledges the person's existence as a free, moral individual bearing the image of God, and treats such as responsible individuals by holding them accountable for their choices.

Retributive punishment will, according to the Bible, accomplish the secondary results that many are trying to achieve through criminal justice systems. Retributive punishment accomplishes reformation within society, for God says that the people will see and learn not to sin. Retribution will protect society against crime. God frequently speaks of punishment, even capital punishment, as removing "the evil from among you." Properly administered, retributive punishment will accomplish the secondary effects of rehabilitation and protection of society. These, however, are not retribution's primary justifications. The basic justification for retribution is the consistent testimony of God's Word. The Bible teaches retributive punishment.

Capital punishment is part of retributive punishment under the Mosaic Law which identifies almost twenty acts as capital crimes. The death penalty for premeditated murder, however, antedates the Mosaic Law by many centuries. In Genesis 9, God established a covenant with Noah as the head of mankind in which he established the death penalty as the judgment for murder. The Noachian Covenant included all mankind in its scope and has never been replaced as the foundational relationship between God and the nations as a whole. After the Deluge, God established another covenant with one individual out of many, Abraham, and later gave Abraham's descendants a more detailed legal code through Moses. The Mosaic Law was in effect over Israel until the death and resurrection of Jesus Christ. The end of the Mosaic Code ended the application of the death penalty for such things as breaking the Sabbath, adultery, and cursing parents. The end of the Law, however, did not terminate capital punishment for murder, for this penalty was established before the Abrahamic Covenant and the Mosaic Code. While there is abundant biblical data showing that the Mosaic Code was limited to a specific group of people and in effect for a limited time, there is no indication that the Noachian Covenant has ended. Consequently, we argue that God still commands governments to exercise capital punishment in the case of murder.

Neither Jesus nor Paul abrogated the death penalty. Jesus accepted the validity of the Mosaic Law, including the death penalty. In the Sermon on the Mount, he refocused the Law on the attitude that lay behind the acts. Murder merited judgment, he taught, but so did hatred which undergirded murder. When confronted with a proven case of adultery in John 8, Jesus did not invoke the death penalty, according to Deuteronomy 22:22–24. Since no one pressed charges against her partner, he dismissed the case and graciously forgave her sin. When Jesus faced Pilate, he did not challenge the governor's authority to have him crucified. He warned Pilate against the misuse of that authority, but affirmed that it had been given to Pilate from above.

Paul likewise accepted the death penalty as a proper exercise of authority by the Roman government and stated his willingness to accept capital punishment if, in fact, he had committed a capital offense. Paul also recognized the government's role as a minister of God's vengeance on evil. Personal vengeance was prohibited, but governments can do what individuals cannot. Believers are not to try to act on behalf of God's wrath; they are to remove themselves and let his proper agents of wrath do their work. Paul acknowledges governmental vengeance through retributive criminal justice systems, and he also acknowledges the magistrate's right to bear the sword. This may well be a symbol of the authority to exercise capital punishment.

Properly administered, capital punishment will deter crime, according to the biblical testimony. It will protect others by providing strong motivation for reformation and by removing violent criminals from society. And, properly carried out, capital punishment is not contrary to the United States Constitution.

However, none of these secondary issues are the foundational justification for capital punishment today. This is found in the Noachian Covenant, which is still in effect today. Consequently, we affirm the validity of the death penalty for murder as a proper exercise of governmental authority. We also affirm the necessity of capital punishment in contemporary societies. There is room for mercy, but there is also a crying need for justice. We can and should hold our governments accountable for obedience to God's demands on them through his covenant to exercise capital punishment for murder.

Against the Death Penalty
John Howard Yoder

Preface
The Shape of My Task
and the Shape of My Presentation

I was first personally introduced to the theme of capital punishment, over thirty years ago, as part of a larger research assignment from the then newly created Institute of Mennonite Studies in Elkhart, Indiana. This was only a fraction of a study of the warrants and the criteria which would tell Christians why we should care and what we should think about the doings of the state. Since then it has not been my privilege to be vocationally involved in ministries or witness related to "corrections," nor in the social sciences which study these matters, but my conviction as to the importance of the matter has not diminished.

I respond therefore with gratitude to the occasion provided by the invitation of Word Publishing and of series editor Vernon Grounds to return to a subject which in thirty years has lost none of its urgency. I must alert the reader that in the space available I cannot undertake the encyclopedic review which might be needed of what has changed in law and criminology since I first wrote on *The Christian and Capital Punishment*. Laws have changed and changed back again, as have the arguments for them. Social science studies have become more complex, in ways I can do no more than cite.

One thing that the years of watching this debate have taught me is that there is no one right place to begin: There is no "scratch" where we might start. The argument is in full swing, with claims of different kinds flowing past each other often without meeting. People who think their view is nothing but "biblical" make unavowed assumptions about facts which the social sciences would need to test. Other people who think their view is purely "scientific" or humanistic make unavowed philosophical or religious assumptions about what is "true" or "good."

It would therefore be a mistake to begin this work of Christian witness, as one might begin a textbook, with the attempt to go back to a nonpartisan beginning and a neutral definition of terms. I must rather accept the fact that the debate is already under way, and must myself enter it in the form it has already taken, in midstream.

These pages can, therefore, not simply state one "side" of a simple pro/con debate. They must take account of how the other "side" of the argument has been promoted, sometimes deceptively, though often sincerely. In so doing, I am, of course, an advocate. I was asked to be that; the book is laid out as a dialogue, guided by the recognition of the very conflictual shape of the conflict of which I have been writing. Yet this bipolar structure may mislead the reader, in several ways:

1. There are more than two positions. There are many not specifically Christian arguments against capital punishment which I shall underplay, not because (especially in our secular democratic context) they are not valuable, but because their theological foundation is not clear. There are refined "yes, but . . ." or "no, but . . ." positions all along the scale between the poles; by no means do only extreme stances have integrity. So the bipolar "debate" format may partly mislead. Those who wish the death penalty retained in the law do not all want it to apply to all possible capital crimes, or to all perpetrators of such crimes.

2. Although I am an advocate, much that I shall report is not the product of bias. Much of the time I shall be having to refer to the literature, to report the "lay of the land," to review the history of the debate, and to survey the views of others, in a relatively objective reportorial mode. I shall be providing background which is not all part of my own argument.

3. Some of the time I shall be selecting for special attention a few specific points, especially in biblical interpretation, to which tradition has given a wrong interpretation. At such points I shall be debating not in the first instance with Professor House, but with the broad stream of

our culture's tradition and its multiple ways of arguing.[1] More than once I shall seek to clarify the course of the conversation by listing the varieties of different meanings that a given word can have, while often its users are unaware of the problems of semantics. Debate has come down to us in legal and institutional terms. Capital punishment is something that governments do, although that was not always the case in history or in the Bible. Our debate must therefore have a legal edge to it. But it should not be only or primarily legal. Christian revulsion at the notion of legal killing is rooted in spiritual experience and in grateful response to the love of God, before it takes shape in critiquing the civil laws. It would be out of order to discuss society's dealing with the offender without asking first how (and why!) God has dealt with our offenses. A Wanda Rempel or a Marietta Yeager, driven by Christian compassion to forgive the murderer of her child and then to reject the death penalty as an institution, incarnates the order of insight and involvement which befits the gospel. It is, therefore, with apologies and under some protest that in much of what I shall be writing I shall be meeting the retentionist argument on the legal level.

There is a widely accepted picture of the shape of the debate which is, if anything, still more misleading than the notion of being able to begin from scratch. This picture is widely held and, therefore, I must openly identify it, and set it aside. It is that support for the death penalty is directly correlated with respecting the Bible, or with historic Christianity, and that support for abolition is therefore a part of unbelief, of disrespect for tradition, or of "humanism" or "liberalism." Obviously, there are some people on both "sides" of that stereotyped dualism; but it does not fairly describe at all the history of the question, nor the position advocated here.

This study does not survey with any fullness the "human" and social-science considerations which count against the death penalty. This is not because I consider them invalid: in a pluralistic society such arguments must be respected. Arguments based on the nature of things or on documented experience cannot ultimately be contrary to arguments derived from revelation. Nonetheless, I underplay them here. I do this because they are already adequately represented in the literature (see the bibliography, pp. 209), because some of those who *believe* their advocacy of the death penalty to be "biblical" are not open to such general humane arguments, *and* because I mean to accentuate the specifically Christian foundation of my most fundamental witness.

It must follow that with no apology I must attend to some matters of detail concerning the language of the Bible and the right way to read ancient texts, which are generally not looked at so closely in the popular literature. I shall seek to do this in an understandable way, but without disrespect for the expertise of those who study such matters in detail.

The material gathered here is brought together from earlier briefer writings produced for other sponsors.[2] I thank those earlier publishers, and the administrators and advisors who assisted my studies.

Moral thinkers are not exempt from the changes in language usage brought about by growing awareness of the sexism built into our language. As far as possible I shall attempt here to decrease the gender tilt of ordinary usage: yet the clumsiness of always needing to say "his or her," or resorting to the ungrammatical singular "they," has not always seemed necessary. Neither for the offenders nor for those who take their lives does reality demand that we routinely say "he or she." After all, this is not a realm where gender-free approaches are pertinent. Executioners are men, almost all of those they execute are men, and the power structure they perpetuate is macho. A feminist critique of the entire correctional enterprise would have enriched our study considerably, but would also have expanded it beyond the scope of the stated project and the competence of the authors.

NOTES

1. Of the numerous contributions to the debate in scholarly biblical terms, that of Bailey (see bibliography) is the strongest recent scholarly case for retention of the penalty of death. When I can allude to it, I shall dispense with other older references.

2. "Capital Punishment and the Bible" in *Christianity Today*, IV/p February 1, 1980, 3–6; *The Christian and Capital Punishment* (Newton, Kan.: Faith and Life Press, 1961); "Capital Punishment and our Witness to Government," *The Mennonite*, June 11, 1963, 390–94.); "The Death Penalty: A Christian Perspective" *The Interpreter* 23/1 January 1979, 3–6; reproduced in Bedau, 1983, pp. 370–75.

1

Where Does the Debate Stand?

I have already pointed out that there is no one proper place at which to begin the treatment of a topic like the social institution of capital punishment. This is not a topic into which one can enter "from scratch," by defining the terms as if they were not already laden with prejudice, and adducing arguments as if all minds were objectively open.

By saying we cannot begin at some neutral beginning I do not mean merely to draw attention to the obvious fact that in any realm involving laws and institutions there is a long history and a large literature. That is certainly also true for the subject of this study. The debate has been going on for centuries. For that reason this book has been provided with a selective bibliography. No attempt can be made to survey the vast debate: the texts listed there under McCafferty, Bedau, and van den Haag all do that quite well. Any serious reader should not be satisfied with what this book can say. It deals little with civil law, with cultural history, and with the diverse legal traditions of different nations, or even of various states within the U.S.

More is meant than that, when I refer to the impossibility of finding a place for the conversation to start. Our subject is by its nature almost sure to mislead. When a society is organized in such a way that certain people are killed—with a good conscience, in the name of the society—that state of things creates a very special kind of institution. By the nature of the case, such an institution does not operate according to ordinary rules. Even if we try to imagine a very simple society, or if anthropologists or archaeologists should be able to dig one up, what it means for the social organism to make standard institutional arrangements to destroy certain of its members is an extremely complex and basic matter, quite difficult to come to grips with.

Stated Rationale versus Real Reasons

It is not clear on the surface of things what the reasons are for that process of killing offenders. Why people *say* they do things—especially when the things they do are exceptional activities, such as killing some people—is not necessarily the real reason they do it. As we shall see later, the anthropological philosopher René Girard claims to have discovered that there is, in fact, a special set of forces at work, which lead a society to hide from itself the real causes for the bloodshed on which people believe the survival of their culture depends. A society deceives itself—through its bards and playwrights, priests and sages—about the primeval vengefulness lying at the base of social order. Girard may be challenged in his reading of the history, but he is certainly right that we give ourselves deceptive and contradictory explanations for why social killing goes on. We properly need to begin with a broad overview of those reasons, religious and otherwise.

There will always be, in anyone's reading of what they think is said by a text of the Bible, a set of presuppositions of which even the people who hold them are not critically aware. Some of these presuppositions are what we call "common sense": they are the unexamined "glasses" through which we experience our life and read a text. Some of the persons most sincerely convinced that they are listening only to the Bible may be the most naively self-deceived about the cultural spectacles they wear. This may happen on both sides of any issue, and it does happen on both sides of this one.

Some would speak of these unquestioned assumptions as "myths" needing to be debunked. But sometimes a "myth" is a figurative way of saying something true, whereas here we are dealing with wrong readings as to matters of fact, or debatable readings as to logic.

One set of these presuppositions are amateur ideas about matters of fact which the social sciences can test. The simplest example of this is the widespread assumption that punishments prevent crime, and that more stringent punishments prevent crime more effectively. Arthur Koestler reports how in England in 1800 a ten-year-old boy was hanged for stealing mail; the judge justified it on the grounds of "the infinite danger of its going abroad into the world that a Child might commit such a crime with impunity."[1]

That judge was taking for granted, in other words, as self-evident fact, that the penalty of death deters: it keeps others from doing the same thing, out of the fear of the same punishment.[2] People first assume that *they* interpret the Bible to be saying the same thing. Before we move on to test that idea in other ways, we must begin by clearing away the most basic misunderstandings.

If we want correctly to understand an ancient text, we need to surface its unstated assumptions, and to test them. Even more should we be critical of our modern "glasses" if the text we are reading is our "Scripture"; i.e., if its account has authority for us. Our culture is far from that of the ancient Near East. If we do not understand the distance, our very effort to take the text "straight" can lead to misunderstanding. What killing a killer is supposed to achieve, according to the thought of the ancient culture underlying some text of Genesis, or Deuteronomy, is not the same as what that English judge quoted above was assuming about the way violence works.[3]

We can then not fairly let the text of the Bible speak for itself without looking at the screen which our modern or medieval presuppositions have put in its way. This "looking at the screen" or "clearing the thicket" will have several parts. We may properly begin, with the issue as I propose to do here, on the level of the uncritical "taken-for grantedness" of the idea that future crimes are prevented by punishing those accused of previous ones. Such "deterrence" is the root reason in the minds of most of those who think the matter already settled. If we look closer, we find that the error of that assumption has several dimensions:

1. *Deterrence was not the basis* for the blood-for-blood demand of primitive cultures. We may argue about whether what those cultures called for was vengeance or expiation or something else. With René Girard we might call it "mimetic desire." When we come to look closer at a few Old Testament texts, we shall come to grips with the specific difference between "ritual" and "law." Numerous angles of approach may

be helpful; we need not choose only one. But what does not fit the ancient facts, or the ancient texts, is the kind of modern pragmatic rationalism which claims that if we threaten people with death for committing X, people will be reasonable and will not commit X.

What was really going on culturally in the ancient origins of the death penalty was something markedly different. What was decisive then was the notion that to kill a killer restored some kind of cosmic moral order. If we today believe in that kind of cosmic order, we may have a logical right to appeal to the ancient examples. In that connection, we shall give close attention to the question of how to read the books of Moses. But one thing ancient worldviews cannot sustain is the theory of deterrence.

2. *Deterrence does not work.* Even when the threat was irrationally disproportionate, as in the bloodthirsty England of which Arthur Koestler wrote, the threat did not deter. When in England around 1800 petty thefts were sanctioned by hanging, there was no lack of people who continued to commit petty thefts and to be hanged for it. Many representative human beings, like ourselves—including petty thieves in England in 1800 and cocaine dealers in the USA in 1991— do not order their lives by rationally maximizing predictable cost-benefit trade-offs in such a way that laws which increase the pain threatened to those who commit harmful actions will prevent those actions from happening. Most of our decisions—especially about wrongdoing—are not guided by computer-like calculations of cost and benefit.[4]

Even less does deterrence "work" in the case of modern capital crimes. Murder is not a normal, rational, goal-oriented, cost-effective human behavior, even if stealing money or selling drugs might be. Many persons who kill are driven by forces of emotion or outright insanity such that no reasoning process, no calculation of the price to pay, takes place when they decide to kill. Some cases are in fact on record where unbalanced persons, lacking the strength of will to kill themselves, have committed murder *because of the death penalty* as an indirect means of suicide.[5]

The other major category of killers are persons at home in the world of crime, for whom the risk of punishment is one of the hazards which add spice to the game. In our society they stand a good chance of not being caught, and if caught, of not being convicted, and if convicted, of not being executed.

Thus far, we have been looking in a common-sense way at whether deterrence "works." Another way to test the theory is statistical. Sociologist

Thorsten Sellin pioneered in this kind of study, comparing the records of states with similar populations, with and without the death penalty. Rhode Island (without) then had a lower crime rate than Connecticut and Massachusetts (with); Michigan (without) lower than Ohio and Indiana (with), Wisconsin (without) lower than Iowa and Minnesota (with). If all the states are compared, the murder rate is over twice as great in states which have (and regularly enforce) the death penalty than in those which do not.[6]

This by no means proves that to abolish the death penalty would of itself reduce the crime rate. It does mean, though, that other considerations—cultural, social, economic, racial—have more to do with determining how much crime will occur than does the presence of a death penalty on the lawbooks. The same cultural values which make life cheap in the eyes of the courts make it cheap in the eyes of the killers.

The punishments thought to be deterrent may, in fact, have the opposite effect. There is statistical evidence that the wide attention given to executions by the public media may incite others to violence or even killing. The potential killer may see himself as represented in the public drama not by the offender who is destroyed but by the authorities whose violence is acted out with approval.[7]

3. *Deterrence, if it did work, would be immoral.* The fundamental moral axiom of Western civilization, as stated in nonsectarian language, is that I should deal with each person—her or his rights, values, needs—as an end in herself or himself, not as a means to some other end. To inflict pain or death on one person *for the sake of* the interests of other persons, interests which it is claimed that that threat will protect, is to sin against that basic rule. Even more, of course, is this the case, when the penalty is disproportionate, as when petty thieving, even by children, was punishable by death.

"... it is a grave moral wrong to treat one person in a way justified solely by the needs of others. To inflict harm on one person in order to serve the purposes of others is to use that person in an immoral and inhumane way, treating him or her not as a person with rights and responsibilities but as a means to other ends. The most serious flaw in the deterrence argument, therefore, is that it is the wrong *kind* of argument."[8]

Immanuel Kant stated this rule most abstractly in the language of Enlightenment philosophy: as cited above, he stated that a person must be treated as an end and not as a means. Yet, it is not a merely "philosophical" rule. Its substance is a paraphrase of the biblical doctrine of the divine image. It *may* be arguable—although hardly in all cases—that in terms of secular social contract philosophy a killer can be claimed to have forfeited his right to have his life protected; but in the biblical vision that right is inalienable. The offender cannot give it away, because it is not his to give; it belongs to God.

Though perhaps sincerely appealed to by the unthinking, the deterrence rationale is thus not really the reason for present practice. If the purpose of killing killers were to frighten others, the executions should be public, as they used to be, and the means of execution should be as painful and disgusting as possible. Yet, the trend is away from this. Executions in the U.S. are not public. There is general embarrassment when, due to clumsy administration of gas or electrocution, the victim is cruelly tortured before dying.

Likewise, if the deterrent theory were to "work," the certainty that every killer will be killed would have to be nearly absolute. Yet, in fact, most killers are not killed; not even most persons convicted of capital offenses are in fact executed.

We thus have to conclude that the language of deterrence is being used by our society to justify, when it is under attack from a moral perspective, action which in fact is caused by a different motivation: namely, vengeance or expiation.

This is not a conclusion; it is a restatement of our starting point. We need to pursue our study further in order to understand the deep cultural drivers behind retribution as an established social institution.

NOTES

1. Koestler (p. 14): "Repeal this law [the death penalty for shoplifting], and I am certain depredations to an unlimited extent would immediately be committed. Repeal this law, and see the contrast—no man can trust himself for an hour out of doors without the most alarming apprehensions that, on his return, every vestige of his property will be swept off by the hardened robber. . . ." Lord Allenborough, Chief Justice of England, in the House of Lords, 1810, cited in Byron E. Eshelman, *Death Row Chaplain* (Englewood Cliffs, N. J.: Prentice-Hall, 1962), 31.

2. To deter is literally to "frighten off," to prevent by fear. The word is used in this proper sense in the following pages. It is the effect which capital

punishment is supposed to have on other actors. There are those, however, for whom "deter" means simply "prevent." Obviously, if a guilty person is killed, *that* person will not kill again. But the word for that should be "prevention."

3. Bailey, 31f and 52, argues, I think rightly, that deterrence was not the motivation for the Mosaic jurisprudence.

4. "After all these years on Death Row, I have come to believe that the only persons the death penalty deters are those who would not be likely to kill anyway," Byron E. Eshelman, *Death Row Chaplain*, 220f.

5. "[Robert] decided he did not want to live, but knew he did not have the courage to kill himself. The thought came to him, after reading about an execution, that if he killed someone else, the state would take his life in return. This particular side effect of the death penalty . . . is revealed in every careful study . . . . Consciously, but more often subconsciously, the mentally adrift use the state as an instrument for suicide," Byron E. Eshelman, *Death Row Chaplain*, p. 127. "I began to trace their criminal deeds as symptoms that began to take form in childhood. . . . Did they have the chance to lead normal lives? Only if it is assumed that such criminals have complete free will to counteract their early conditioning and emotional stunting can a rational case be put forward for vindictive punishment and the death penalty. If this cannot be assumed, then the foundation crumbles under every argument in favor of capital punishment." Byron E. Eshelman, *Death Row Chaplain*, 62.

6. Sellin's state-by-state comparison studies were done in the 1950s, and updated in 1980. The evidence keeps changing, as the laws and practices of state courts change (some states have capital punishment laws on the books but execute no one). Likewise, the tools of statistical analysis get much more complex (cf. the fuller statistical work of Klein et al., pp. 138ff in Bedau, 1982). The strongest argument on one side is the claim of Isaac Ehrlich, "The Deterrent Effect of Capital Punishment . . . ," *American Economic Review* 65 (1975), 397ff, according to whose complex argument every time a killer is killed several lives are saved. It provoked responses in the *Yale Law Journal* 85 (1975–76), 164–227 and 359–69, as in Bedau, 1975, 372–95. Despite the extended attention the deterrent argument is given on both sides, it is a distraction from the profound levels of the debate. A person who believes on profound religious or philosophical grounds that the death penalty is immoral would not admit that the possibility of deterring other killings would suffice to justify it. A person who believes on religious or philosophical grounds that every killer must in turn be killed will not be dissuaded by evidence to the effect that it does not deter. On both sides of the debate, the theme of deterrence is a second-order or ancillary argument.

7. Cf. William J. Bowers; "The Effect of Executions is Brutalisation, Not Deterrence," in Haas and Inciardi (see bibliography), 49–89.

8. David Hoekema (see bibliography), 339.

2

Noah's Covenant and
the Purpose of Punishment

The case for the death penalty as an institution in modern societies has several quite different roots. Different advocates appeal to quite different reasons in its favor. We have already noted in our beginning pages the need to look at them one by one, each in its own terms. The first reason, as most people read it, is the notion of prevention by threat, or "deterrence," which we have already looked at and seen to be deceptive.

The first religiously based argument, on the other hand, for most Christians, comes from the story of Noah. As we range around the argument, seeking the most solid ground, this is one obviously right place to begin. It appears literally to be a direct divine command:

> Whosoever sheds the blood of Man
> In Man shall his blood be shed
> For in the image of God
> He made Man.[1] (Gen. 9:6)

Does This Text Prove What It Has Been Assumed To?

The first task of the biblical interpreter, as I already said, is not to read a text as if "from scratch," or as if its meanings were self-evident to every

119

well-intentioned reader, but rather to protect the text from misuse, even to "liberate" its original meaning from the deposit of interpretations which have already been laid over it by centuries of readers. To say this is not to suggest that earlier readers were dishonest or insincere. It is merely to take seriously the fact that they were prisoners of their cultures, as we are of ours, even as the text we are seeking to read was the product of its own culture.

We need to make a self-conscious effort to understand the focus of the worldview implicit in the culture from which any ancient text comes to us. Some tend to read a text like this as if it were legislation, providing, prehistorically, at no particular time but with validity for all times, that there should be a particular institution, equivalent to what we call the state, the basis for civil law, to protect threatened social values.

God's covenant with Noah was not that. We need to step back from such modernizing assumptions if we are to have any hope of understanding how the sanctity of life was really understood in the ancient Israelite setting where these words were first recited.

"Recited" is the right description of how this ancient text was originally used. This rhythmic quatrain (further rhythmic in that in Hebrew the words "blood" and "man" rhyme) is not part of a code of laws, though such codes did exist at that time in the ancient Near East. It was formulated as oral lore, recited by sages and priests, repeated by the old, and remembered by the young. It is part of the deep symmetry of things, fitting in with the seasonal, rhythmic reliability of nature:

> As long as earth lasts
> sowing and reaping
> cold and heat,
> summer and winter
> day and night
> shall cease no more. (Gen. 8:22 JB)

This is not legislation for a government to apply. It is wisdom, a prediction, a description, of how things are in fact, in primitive and ancient societies. The nature of things did not come to be this way only because God said these words, as if without the words, or before God spoke them, matters would have been different. That is true of some kinds of human laws, nonexistent before, which come into being only when voted by a legislature or promulgated by a king or other authority.

We also err when we tend to read this text as if the defense of life through the threat to life were a new arrangement, established only after the Flood. It hardly can be taken that way, as the text of Genesis now stands.[2] Things were already that way before the covenant with Noah; in fact, that was the way it was as soon as the first murder was reported. That arrangement is already presupposed in the account of Cain, in Genesis 4. There the first murderer, called to account for the life of the brother he had killed, said:

My punishment is greater than I can bear;
behold : you drive me from this ground.[3]
I must hide from you and be a fugitive and wanderer over the earth.
Whoever comes across me will kill me. (Gen. 4:13f JB)

What Cain feared was, as it were, a defensive reflex of society as a whole, of "everyone who sees me." There is no account of there having been a previous divine command demanding blood for blood. The response of Yahweh to the jeopardy under which Cain saw himself was to intervene, to protect his life by a "mark"[4] and to announce the threat of retaliation. Thus, the first intervention of God in Genesis, counter to the ordinary reading, is not to demand that murder be sanctioned by sacrificial killing, but to protect the life of the first murderer. Far from demanding the death penalty for murder, Yahweh saved Cain from it. That is the first and the most characteristic action of the God of the Bible with regard to our subject.[5]

Yet, the pattern of violence continued and escalated out of all proportion. Cain's descendant, Lamech, boasted:

I have slain a man for wounding me,
a young man for striking me.
If Cain is avenged sevenfold,[6]
truly Lamech seventy-seven-fold! (Gen. 4:23f.)

This is the normal pattern; fallen humanity responds to evil with *escalating* vengeance. Primitive peoples show the same pattern as

Lamech, from the intertribal wars of Borneo through the bloody gang justice of the Sicilian hills and the American underworld, to the proverbial "feudin' hillbillies" of the Appalachians. Each *particular* act of vengeance is thought of as "setting things right" or as "defending the peace," but in fact the spiral escalation of vengeance and counter-vengeance raises the toll of suffering brought about by any one offense, far beyond any proportion to the original damage done.

Having opened our minds to the awareness that the reason for primitive revenge was not the same as our modern arguments, we can and should move on to note what is different about the agents of the action.

The ancient quatrain does not say who the "man" is who shall shed the killer's blood. Certainly, it was not a constitutional government by means of a trial by judge or jury. Historians tell us that it was the next of kin, called "the avenger" (*goel*, the same Hebrew word as "redeemer") who executed family-based vengeance. The mechanism of retaliation, once unleashed, had to run its course. Later laws spell this out. If a corpse was found with no way to know whom to punish, very special ceremonies were needed on the part of the elders of the nearest town to "cover" them against the blood-vengeance which was due (Deut. 21:1–8). A person who killed accidentally could be protected only by taking refuge in one of six designated "cities of refuge" and staying there for the entire life of the high priest (Num. 35:11–28, cf. Deut. 4:42f; 19:1–10). No ransom was possible for blood guilt, even when the death was accidental (Num. 35:32f). Nor was bloodshed the only occasion for such sanctions. Death was the penalty as well for dozens of other offenses (cf. below p. 207).

There are others who read the Noah story as if it belonged in Exodus or Leviticus, as part of a body of rules set out to govern the particular nation of Israel, to be established much later in the land of Canaan, in the light of the sovereignty of Yahweh, in whose name Moses was to make of his mixed multitude (Exod. 12:38) a nation. It was not that. When that civil legislation did arise later, it too was to have provision for the death penalty, as we shall see, but not for the same reasons, and for many other kinds of offenses.

The context of Genesis 9 is that of ritual sacrifice. The anthropologist will call it "cultic" or "sacred." These four rhyming lines about human killing do not stand alone. In the same breath, the text had just been describing animal sacrifice. As contrasted with the vegetarian arrangement implied before the Deluge, animal flesh may now be eaten, but only subject to a ceremonial sense of the holiness of animate life as such, which is represented by the blood:

> Every living and crawling thing shall provide food for you
>> no less than the foliage of plants
> I give you everything, with the exception
>> that you must not eat flesh with the life
> —that is, the blood—in it
> I will demand an account of your life blood
> I will demand an account from every beast and from man
> I will demand an account of every man's life
>> from his fellow man
> he who sheds man's blood. . . .(Gen. 9:6 JB)

The setting of our text is thus the account, after the Flood, of God's authorizing the killing of animals for human consumption. In the context, it is evident that the subject of the passage is sacrifice. The sacredness of human life is described in the same breath with God's exclusive claim on the blood of the sacrificially slaughtered beasts, and as an extension of the same. To kill animals for food is not like picking fruit from a tree, pulling turnips from a garden, or cutting wheat in a field. It is an interference with the dynamics of animate life, represented by the flow of blood through the body, which humans share with the animal world. Every killing is a sacrifice, for the life of the animal, represented by its blood, belongs to God. To kill an animal is a ritual act; the blood belongs not to the killer but to God. There is no "secular" slaughtering of animals in ancient Israel. The blood of the animal is given to God by being sprinkled on the altar or poured out on the ground. The act of eating that meat is an act of communion with God. The provision for shedding the blood of a human killer is part of the same sacrificial worldview.

The closest approximation in the later Mosaic laws to the sense of the sacred which sanctions killing in Genesis 9 is the prohibition of serving another god (Deut. 13:1–16). This text emphasizes the responsibility of any individual to be the agent of retaliation, even against one's closest kin. A whole town could need to be slaughtered and even the property destroyed.

Other ancient societies, primitive or highly developed, used human sacrifice for many other purposes. The God who renews with Noah his life-saving covenant with humanity permits human sacrifice—for that is what is prescribed here—*only* on one specific grounds, namely, to correct for a previous wrongful taking of human life.

Thus, it is not at all the case that in addressing Noah God intervenes to make blood vengeance a duty, when it had not been so before. The pattern was already old. It is then a mistake to read the word to Noah as if it were a command, ordering its hearers to do something which they would otherwise not have done. It is not that: it is a simple description of the way things already are, an accurate prediction of what does happen, what will happen, as surely as summer is followed by winter, seedtime by harvest. That killers are killed is the way fallen society works; it is not a new measure which God introduced after the Deluge to solve a problem that had not been there before, or for which God had not yet found a solution. It rather restates, as a fact and as a prediction, in the framework of the authorization now being granted to sacrifice and eat animals, that the sacredness of human life, already stated when God had saved the life of the murderer Cain, still stands. Spoken just at the place in the story where the killing of animals is for the first time authorized, the point of God's word in Genesis 9 is to reiterate the prohibition of the killing of humans.[7]

Motives and Meanings for Primitive Revenge

The careful cultural historian will have to ask at this point which of several descriptions or explanations best fits the primitive fact of blood revenge. We cannot yet review fully the several answers to this question as they are operative in modern debate,[8] but we must at least recognize the wrongness of leaping past it to too simple an answer. What were the possible meanings for Cain's contemporaries or Noah's descendants of shedding a killer's blood?

1. It might be more precisely described as eradication, getting rid of the source of trouble. The Old Testament speaks of "purging" evil from

the Israelite people.[9] This would be the social equivalent of what white blood cells do to microbes or what exterminators do to vermin. The organism defends itself against a threat by removing whatever threatens. The threatening organism has no rights of its own. It is removed because it is bad, not because of a particular bad behavior.

2. It might be described as imitation, *mimesis*. I do to you what you did to my friend, not out of some general theory of social hygiene but rather, primitively, reflexively, because it does not occur to me do anything else.[10] You "have it coming."

3. It might be understood as intimidation. If as a general pattern it is known that those who harm others are harmed in return, this may keep them from doing it. This interpretation has several levels of meaning. One is the more narrow, mental, and therefore more modern sense. The thought is that an individual, premeditating an evil deed, will "think twice" about the cost, and will therefore renounce the evil deed on cost/benefit grounds. "Deterrence" is another modern term for this. Intimidation also has a less mental, more primitive, more "educational" sense. The generalized practice of avenging certain offenses, it is held, tends to be one way a society has of trying to teach people what deeds are offensive, not to be considered, therefore hoping to make it less likely that they will occur.

4. Both of the above concepts, "imitation" and "intimidation," can be understood to be founded in "retaliation." The root *-tal-* means "such" or "like." One may believe that God or the gods or "the moral order" should be understood in terms of a kind of balancing exercise, whereby each harmful act needs to be "paid back" or "set right" by another harmful act of the same kind and dimensions. When the "moral order" is thought of in analogy to a courtroom, we may also speak of the *talion* as "vindication,"[11] but in the old Semitic setting the courtroom is not the best symbol for that.

5. None of the above is quite what we mean when we use the word *revenge*. Usually the term *revenge* connotes an element of passion.[12] To do something "with a vengeance" suggests disregard for proportion, or for limits or barriers. It reaches beyond "eye for eye." A vengeful society, or the individual avenger, demands retaliation, claims moral legitimacy for the vindictive act, and may draw emotional satisfaction from carrying it out. Some would avow "anger" as a valid description of the

motivation that is at work in so punishing the offender, and some would disavow it. Others would say that there is no anger in justice.

6. None of the above is quite what we mean by "expiation." This term points past the harm done to the social order, to the offense against the will of God or the gods. The divine anger must be placated, or the cosmic moral order must be set back in balance, the offender must "pay." In some religious and cultural settings the divine wrath is understood very anthropomorphically: God gets "mad." In others, the claim is that the "balance" needing to be restored by punishment is quite dispassionate, objective like a court's judgment, and holy.

Certainly, these several possible characterizations of why killers are killed are not all the same. The differences are significant. We shall come back later to try to disentangle them more abstractly, as part of our review of the modern debate. But now we want merely to understand the Noah story. Which of them most adequately describes the facts? Which of them is morally most or least acceptable?

On the above scale, most of those who today hold the death penalty to be morally justified would hold to a somewhat sanitized, modernized version of "legislation" combined with "intimidation." This is what we previously referred to under the broader heading of "deterrence." It has the least basis in the ancient text.

On the other hand, most historians studying where the legal killing of humans actually came from in ancient society, including ancient Israel, would point to one of the more angry versions of "vengeance" combined with "imitation." Journalists watching in our own times the public outcry after some particularly brutal killing would agree with the historians.

Our debate to this day is skewed by the difference between these two interpretations. Is killing a killer a vengeful action against the evildoer himself? Or is it the restoration of divine moral balance through sacrifice?

For now, this first overview of the spectrum of reasons is intended only to provoke the reader's vigilance. We need to be warned against the assumption that we know easily just which of those meanings the Genesis text originally had for its first hearers and against the assumption that the ancient meaning has any direct connection with the reasons for the modern death penalty.

The provision of Genesis 9:6 is thus not a moral demand, saying that for every pain inflicted there must be another pain inflicted to balance the scales of justice. It is not an educational demand, teaching the offender (or destroying the offender in order to teach others) a lesson to the effect that crime does not pay. It is not a political order describing how to administer a healthy city.

The order underlying the words in question is ritual; human life, human blood is sacred—whoever sheds it forfeits his own. The demand for that "forfeiting" is not vengeance on the part of the victim's family, although it easily degenerates into that; it is the organic society living in immediate awareness of the divine quality of human life. The death which sanctions death is ceremonial, celebrative, ritual.

The killing of a killer is not a civil, nonreligious matter. It is a sacrificial act. The blood—i.e., the life—of every man and beast belongs to God. To respect this divine ownership means, in the case of animals, that the blood of a sacrificed victim is not to be consumed. For humans, it means that there shall be no killing. If there is killing, the offense is a cosmic, ritual, religious evil, demanding ceremonial compensation. It is not a moral matter; in morality a second wrong does not make a right. It is not a civil, legislative matter: it is originally stated in a setting where there is no government.

Ritual Worldview and Cultic Change

One way that the ritual worldview differs from our own is that there is no concern for personal accountability. The death penalty applied to an ox which gored a man. It applied to unintended or accidental killing. If the ritual worldview of Genesis 9:6 were to be applied to our culture literally, there would be no provision for exculpating minors or the mentally ill, no separating of degrees of homicide according to intention. We would execute the contractor whose bridge collapses, the engineer whose train is wrecked, the auto driver whose brakes malfunction, if death results. For every death, blood must flow.

Christians in recent centuries, in order to attempt to understand and describe how the laws of the Old Testament ought to be respected since Christ, have proposed to divide them into civil, ceremonial, and moral laws. They then explain that the "moral" laws continue to apply in all times, but that the ceremonial ones are abrogated when the sacrificial order is fulfilled in Christ as the final sacrifice and the final high priest.

Some of the civil laws, it is held, should apply to modern states, and others were intended only for the government of ancient Israel. This threefold (really fourfold) distinction may help to organize our thought, but careful study of the death penalty provisions of the books of Moses makes it clear that the distinction is alien to that world.

The covenant given to Noah involved no such distinction either, but the elements we call "moral" and "civil" were not stated, not separated. We saw that Genesis 9 speaks of the blood of animals and of fellow humans as belonging to God—certainly a sacrificial concept. The covenant given through Moses was no less holistic. Just as the Christ who was to come would be prophet, priest, and king all at once, so the covenant established through Moses was moral, ceremonial, and civil all at once, not one of them in distinction from the others. For centuries after Moses there was in Israel no king, nothing specific to call "civil."

The distinction between different types of law has served, although in an indirect, illogical way, to make room for a valid point. The valid point, which these distinctions alluded to, is that there was going to have to be change over time in how the laws would apply, and that in those changes the sacrifice of Christ was to make the biggest difference.

It is the clear testimony of the New Testament, especially of the Epistle to the Hebrews, that the ceremonial requirements of the Old Covenant find their end—both in the sense of fulfillment and in the sense of termination—in the high-priestly sacrifice of Christ. "Once for all" is the good news. Not only is the sacrifice of bulls and goats, turtledoves and wheatcakes at an end; the fact that Christ died for our sins, once for all, the righteous one for the godless (Heb. 9:26–28, 1 Pet. 3:18), puts an end to the entire expiatory system, whether it be enforced by priests in Jerusalem or by executioners anywhere else.[13]

Thus, by asking where killing began, and finding in the stories of both Cain and Noah what is said and what is not said there, we have been led to the most precise statement of the specifically Christian reason for the death penalty's being set aside. There are other reasons as well, more widely effective in our world, in which Anglo-Saxon democracy has spelled out the implications of the Hebrew and Christian heritage, but this is the reason closest to the heart of the gospel.

That shedding blood exposes the killer to killing is expiation in the name of the cosmic order. The death of Christ is the end of expiation.

Noah's Covenant and the Purpose of Punishment

The Ritual Nature of Social Behavior

To kill a killer is a ritual act, we have begun to see, not primordially or only in a political sense. When people gather for the funeral of a public figure, when they build a wall around their house or buy an assault gun, when they fly a flag or take off their hats, the event is not adequately interpreted by asking about a specified moral imperative, or about a pragmatic social goal. We have just attempted briefly to explain something of this sense of the sacred as it shows in the Noah story; now let us note that it is still the case today.

When society takes a life, the action is, obviously, not being undertaken for the well-being of that person. Counter to the general moral rule, most simply stated in modern times by Immanuel Kant, that a person is always to be treated as an end and not as a means, when a person is killed, that cannot be an action in that person's interest. It is a public ritual, celebrated in the interest of others, in the interest of the society's controlling elite and those who support them, and their vision of the society's well-being.

When a parent or a teacher spanks a child, when an offender is put in prison or fined, it can be *claimed* that it is done in order to "teach" that guilty person something. Even then, the careful psychologist or social scientist will warn us that the real "learning" resulting from that event is probably something else. A child trained by spanking may grow up to become a teenage gangster or an abusive parent. What beating a child teaches most effectively may well be less "don't get into the cookie jar" than "might makes right," or "if you cannot reason, use force." The same may be true of other punishments as well. The petty pilferer sent to prison may learn there the skills of the professional burglar.

So the claim to "teach him a lesson" is often factually wrong. Nevertheless, it may be sincerely so intended. The sincere intention may be that the offender himself should learn that "crime does not pay," so that he does not repeat the offense. The time behind bars may lead him to think differently.

Rationales for Rehabilitation

This notion of changing the offender, ordinarily called "rehabilitation," *can* be given as a serious reason for depriving the

129

offender of his liberty. He is shown how wrong his actions were. He may become convinced that he is under society's control. He may be led to promise (sincerely or not) that he will not repeat the offense. He may be given time to show by his actions that his promise to behave is credible, and he may even be taught a trade or helped to finish school. This is why prisons were once called "penitentiaries," places to repent. Some persons, after a prison term, do not return to crime. As long as the prospect of a future life in freedom is real, there is *some* chance that this may succeed. Yet even in these cases it is not clear that the time in prison or other kind of punishment is what made the most difference in a person's readiness to become a good member of society.

But when the line of life is crossed, the entire "teach-a-lesson" rationale becomes a lie. The only persons who can "learn" from a lethal public ritual are the others.

- the victims of the past crime (if they are alive) or their relatives can take comfort from the fact that the person who hurt them has been hurt in return: "vengeance" is the ordinary word for this. Vengefulness, taking comfort in the pain of others, is not a good moral quality in an individual, but some feel that it becomes right when the killing is done by the authorities.
- those who stand to lose by a crime are reassured that it may be less likely to happen to them—although this confidence in the "deterrent" effect is as we have seen often mistaken.
- persons who have not committed a crime should be warned that they should not think of doing so, out of the fear that they may be caught and punished. Yet, in fact, the limitations of our enforcement system do not make that threat very real in the minds of most potential offenders.
- the civil authorities celebrate and reinforce their posture of social control. In the Aryan feudal roots of our common law, the authority to dispose of the life of one's subjects was what defined a lord's sovereignty. The killer claims to be the instrument of God; he celebrates that his authority to rule is legitimate, by having the right to destroy some of his subjects.

The purpose thus far of our itemizing a few of the diverse modes of motivation has not been to be complete, but only to be broad enough to open for the reader a sense of the complexity of things, and of the inadequacy of simple explanations.

NOTES

1. The noun translated "man" (Hebrew *adam*) here is generic; it means humankind. The Hebrew reader's mind is thrown back to the beginning of chapter 2, where *adam* meant the human race, without gender division or individuation. That Creation narrative was the only place where God's "image" had previously been referred to.

2. Expert Scripture scholarship has projected diverse hypotheses as to the original dates and original authorship of the several strands of the Mosaic literature. That speculation would call into question some simple arguments based on the assumption that a text like that of Genesis was originally a literary unity. There is, however, no serious scholarly claim according to which Genesis 9 would be older than Genesis 4.

3. The ground is personified. "The voice of your brother's blood cries to me from the ground" (4:10); the metaphor of "blood" for life is the same as in chap. 9. Yet the "cry" of the blood is not to be satisfied. God intervenes to save the murderer.

4. Patristic symbolic theology speculated that the "sign" given to Cain to protect him was *tau* or the cross. Biblical scholars hypothesize that it may have been the trace of a tatoo worn by metalworkers; in the ancient world smelting was thought of as a secret stolen from the gods of the underworld (Bailey, 40).

5. JHWH (usually pronounced "Yahweh") is the proper name of God. "Lord" in the AV and in Jewish piety is a reverent substitution. Jehovah and Yahweh are hypothetical reconstructions of the name. Bailey (39 and 107) suggests that Yahweh made a mistake; that if vengeance against Cain had been permitted, then "violence in the earth" would not have escalated so as to necessitate the Deluge. This would take more argument than either Bailey or Genesis provides. Genesis 6:6 says that what God regretted was having created mankind, not having protected Cain. Bailey also makes much of the claim (40, 70) that narrative texts should not be taken as bearing moral instruction. This is an assertion without an argument. Of course each genre of literature should be read in its own terms. Bailey would have done well to distinguish more than he does between Genesis 9 and the Mosaic civil code, or between "moral" and "civil" texts. But narrative can be the vehicle of moral instruction, especially in settings called *etiological*, i.e., texts which deal with why and how things came to be, or in texts exhibiting God's or Jesus' character.

6. Lamech's reference to Cain should not mislead us to think that he was escalating what had been said before by Yahweh. (a) The vengeance threatened in Genesis 4:15 was to be inflicted by Yahweh, but Lamech avenged himself; (b) the threat of 4:15 was successful in deterring harm to Cain, and was not carried out.

7. Some have argued that "by man shall his blood be shed" is a simple future rather than an imperative; a prediction but not an authorization. That is

too little. God avows that the retributive process is under his rule: "I will require a reckoning." Yet, what God thus owns is an extant practice; he does not create a new institution nor decree a new duty.

8. I shall describe the variety of views more fully on pp. 156ff.

9. Bailey, 32.

10. We shall see below how the ethnologist René Girard uses "mimesis" as a far-reaching interpretation of the origins of violence and of government.

11. See pp. 000: The analysis of the texts sometimes is thought to teach most firmly the divine demand for symmetrical retaliation.

12. Under "retribution" we shall return later to the question of emotion.

13. Cf. Karl Barth (in bibliography) Vol. III/4, p. 442f.: "Which category of particularly great sinners is exempted from the pardon effected on the basis of the death penalty carried out at Calvary? Now that Jesus Christ has been nailed to the cross for the sins of the world, how can we still use the thought of expiation to establish the death penalty?"

3

A Second Look at "An Eye for an Eye"

Before we move from ancient Israel back to modernity, we may be helped by one other close textual study, following up a notion of which many think that it is a timeless and universal principle. It is widely assumed (rather than being argued with self-critical care) that the death penalty is one part of a broader foundational logic of equal retaliation which God generally demands or commands as the basic meaning of "justice." We shall look later at the notion of equal retribution, tit for tat, as a claimed universal philosophical truth; here we may be helped by looking closely at the texts in the Old Testament where many think it is expressed.

Because Jesus referred to it in the Sermon on the Mount, as one of the traditional teachings which he was calling his hearers to recognize that the righteousness of the kingdom of God would transcend, we tend to think that the rhyme-like rule:

> an eye for an eye
> a tooth for a tooth

is a very important part of the Hebrew heritage, or even more than that, a part of the definition of divine justice.[1] It is, in fact, not that, and that fact is worth pursuing.

This rule appears only three times in the entire body of Mosaic legislation, never in a context that is textually central. Let us look at each of them carefully. In Exodus 21:24–27 it is cited as background for the special case of a woman's being wounded while two men are fighting. If the woman is pregnant and the injury causes her to miscarry, the compensation shall be fixed by the court. Apparently, the life of the fetus can be compensated for as an economic value. But if the woman dies, the penalty shall be

> life for life;
> eye for eye;
> tooth for tooth;
> hand for hand;
> foot for foot;
> burn wound for burn wound;
> knife wound for knife wound;
> whip wound for whip wound.

It is striking that only the first pair of nouns is in any way pertinent to the context. The rest of the dictum was repeated from memory, just because it was part of the oral legal lore of the time. It is recited as a celebration of the poetic fittingness of letting every punishment fit the crime, one more reminder of the ancient near eastern vision of deep cosmic symmetry, even though it is of no use for the present case. We note that *if* the rule is applied literally in this case, the death penalty is here to be imposed for an *accidental* killing. As elsewhere in the sacred worldview, whether the killing was intentional or not is less important than in our time.

In Leviticus 24:19–22 the setting is narrative: an inquiry is being addressed to Yahweh. The people are petitioning for an oracle regarding the punishment they should inflict for a particular act of blasphemy. The answer given them by the oracle is that the blasphemer should be stoned by the whole community; but then the statement of that command is followed by a series of others:

> if a man kills any man he must die;
> if a man kills an animal he must make restitution for it:
> a life for a life;
> if a man injures his neighbor,

what he did must be done to him:
broken limb for broken limb
eye for eye
tooth for tooth;
as the injury inflicted,
so must be the injury suffered.

Then the narrative goes on to recount the stoning of the blasphemer by the sons of Israel. The text is again odd, in that the list of offenses and punishments is not pertinent at all to the question put to Yahweh, and further odd in that the one particular offense involved in the framing narrative is not dealt with by the same rule. The penalty for cursing God is not to be cursed by God but to be stoned by people.

The third occurrence of the dictum is, on more careful examination, not on the same subject either. In fact, it formally contradicts the general notion of retaliation. The context in Deuteronomy 19:19–21 is the rules of evidence in a court. More than one witness is always needed to find someone guilty.[2] The penalty for the crime of perjury is that he who commits it shall be subjected to whatever the false accuser was asking to have done to the falsely accused. There is an element of symmetry:

deal with him as he would have dealt with his brother;

yet that does not mean that the false accuser should be punished by being falsely accused. It rather means that he is to be treated as if he had been fairly found guilty of what he was unfairly accusing his brother of:

life for life,
eye for eye,
tooth for tooth,
hand for hand,
foot for foot.

We can summarize: In each of the three occurrences, the list of pairs is drawn in on the edge of the treatment of some other subject. In none of them is it the center of the passage. In none of the three cases is it presented as revelation. It is not reported as an oracle presenting new information. (In the Leviticus 24 case it is alluded to within the text of an oracle, but logically it is not limited to that case nor is it applied to it literally.) In none of the three cases does the "eye-for-eye" rule actually dictate what happens. In neither of the two references to "life for life" is the loss of one's own life the penalty for murder.

The lists of pairs are quoted as a reminiscence of a self-evident, already known, easily remembered folk wisdom, a sense of poetic symmetry, taken for granted whenever it applies. It never needs to be explained. The *lex talionis*[3] is then best understood not as a new and central revelation of the demands of the covenant, but as a common-sense, natural, pre-Mosaic rule of thumb, a distillation of the mimetic reflex at the root of all social sanctions. There is nothing Mosaic or Hebraic about it.

Those who are concerned to explain how Jesus could in the same discourse say "I have not come to dissolve the Law but to fulfill it," and then go on to set aside "an eye for an eye" as no longer adequate, have usually argued that the provision for symmetry in the Mosaic texts had the concrete meaning of a restraint on vengeance which, if not thus limited, would naturally escalate (after the model of Yahweh in Genesis 4:15 or Lamech in Genesis 4:24). Then the concrete meaning was: "For an eye *no more than* an eye, for a tooth *no more than* a tooth." Thus, the symmetry rule already represented restraint. It was a first step in the direction which Jesus then "fulfilled" by taking the concern for limits to its logical conclusion.

This is a very reasonable argument, especially when we note in how many places elsewhere in the Mosaic laws the penalty of death is, in fact, disproportionate. The consistent application of the rule of *talion* would thus be less lethal than the Mosaic rules as a whole.

This interpretation also fits with the way in which the other five "but I say to you" antitheses of Matthew 5 seem uniformly to "go farther in the same direction" beyond what is cited from the "law," rather than contradicting it.[4] Yet, the three particular *talion* texts we are here concerned with do not make explicit this *no-more-than-one-eye* argument. The argument has validity, but it must be made on the basis of our general understandings of the place of more-than-equal retaliation in all ancient law.

A Second Look at "An Eye for an Eye"

It is noteworthy that there is in the Mosaic literature nothing of what is called "indirect talion." Other laws of that period provided, for example, that if a house collapsed and killed the owner's son, the builder's son should be killed in return. There is in Hebrew law no such interest in symmetry for its own sake.[5] There is no notion of lying to a liar, raping a rapist, or stealing from a thief. In most of the several provisions for the death penalty in the Mosaic laws[6] there is no such symmetry.

The appetite for imposing symmetrical suffering is thus a natural reflex in primitive cultures, poetically apt but not always applicable. It is not a revelation either from an oracle of Yahweh or from universal moral reason. It is more an esthetic imperative than a moral one. It is a standard cultural reflex rather than a prescriptive guide. Jesus explicitly sets it aside.

NOTES

1. A striking specimen of this symbolic meaning of the phrase is its use as the title in the book by Wright (see bibliography). Evidently the publishers considered the phrase to be highly representative of the ethical problem posed by the Old Testament (the British original edition was entitled, *Living as the People of God*). Yet in the text of his study Wright does not interpret at all any of the three "eye for eye" passages. He even refers only very fleetingly (166) to the entire notion of retribution.

2. Also in Deuteronomy 17:6 and Numbers 35:30. The New Testament refers to this rule of evidence: Matt. 18:16, 1 Tim. 5:19, Heb. 10:28, and metaphorically in 1 John 5:7. Rabbinic judicial practice, already by the first century, was very reluctant to condemn anyone on circumstantial evidence.

3. The very currency of a Latin term for the concept of retaliation (see 125) confirms that it is part of a general pagan social wisdom, not intended nor received as a new disclosure of revealed righteousness.

4. I myself made the same argument in my *The Original Revolution*, 44. I do not withdraw the point today, but it did over-value the extent to which the original use of "eye for eye" etc. was stated as if it were divine law.

5. Bailey (27–30) lists numerous other ways in which the Mosaic rules and practices were conditioned, in ways we might call "humane," in contrast to the rules of the environing societies. Similar contrasts are pointed out by Wright (166ff).

6. Bailey's detailed count (pp. 19–22) is seventeen. See p. 207, my own list.

137

4

Jesus and the Civil Order

The only clear reference to be found in the New Testament to the infliction of death as a penalty is in John's Gospel (8:1–11). A woman was brought to Jesus with the report that she was known to be guilty of adultery.[1] "Moses has ordered us in the Law to condemn women like this to death by stoning. What have you to say?" The intention of the "scribes and pharisees," we are told, was to put Jesus to a test; i.e., they were not really looking for help with defining or doing God's will. Their primary motivation was not to wipe out adultery. They were, rather, challenging Jesus to continue to exercise the authority he had been claiming while teaching in the Temple (chap. 7). Jesus did not evade the challenge. We may, therefore, rightly take his response as bearing on our study.

Jesus could well have pointed out that "Moses" (i.e., the Law, in Leviticus 20 and Deuteronomy 22) does not say that a woman should be condemned without the man with whom she was caught in the act. Why did they bring him the woman without the man? Jesus could have made an important point about male sexism and the victimizing of women. But he chose not to.

Jesus could well have challenged the factual accuracy of their report about the offense, as the law requires, and as a judge would have done. He did not. Nor did he deny that the provision for death was in the Law. Nor did he cite in the woman's defense, as a rabbinic court would have, the longstanding hesitancy of Jewish local authorities, for several centuries already, to inflict the death penalty. He did not (explicitly) make the point which according to the same Gospel "the Jews" later argued before Pontius Pilate (18:31), namely, that under the Roman rules currently in effect Jewish authorities did not have the right to put anyone to death. All of these responses would have been fitting. In a full account, we should need to consider them all. Jesus, however, preferred to make two other points, to which we should also give priority.

"Let him that is without sin cast the first stone."[2] If the death penalty is understood as an act of God (as it certainly was in ancient Israel), then the judge and executioner must be morally above reproach. "When they heard this they went away one by one, beginning with the eldest. . . ." Why was it the eldest who first disqualified themselves? The Christian challenge to the death penalty properly begins where Jesus does, by challenging the self-ascribed righteousness of those who claim the authority to kill others.

Secondly, Jesus applied to this woman's offense his authority to forgive. He did not deny her guilt, but he absolved it as far as punishment was concerned, and liberated her from its power over her: "Sin no more." He recognized no differentiation between the religious and the civil, according to which the sin could be forgiven, yet punitive justice should still have to be done.

John's concern in telling this story was, of course, not to provide his readers with new information about the legality of capital punishment.[3] His testimony was about the authority of Jesus as the One uniquely sent by the Father. That is just our point. We are not studying law for its own sake; we are learning that the saviorhood of Jesus applies to law, and to social punishment for sin, no less than to prayer. Jesus as the forgiver of sin not only removes sin's power over the sinner's behavior but also its power to dictate guiltiness and demand punishment.

Jesus' Good News Condones the Lesser Moral Level of the Civil Order

Like the divorce which Deuteronomy 24 condoned, like the distortions of the law which Jesus corrected in Matthew 5, like the institution of slavery, and the oppressive presence in Judea and Galilee of the Roman

Empire which neither Jesus nor Paul rose up against, capital punishment is one of those infringements on the holy will of God in society, which can claim a certain formal legitimacy. The gospel does not immediately eliminate such from secular society, since, being noncoercive, the gospel cannot "rule the world" in that way. Yet, to condone the way things stand is not approval: "from the beginning it was not so" (Matt. 19:8). Jesus said that literally about the Mosaic provision for divorce; but the Christians of the apostolic generation thought in the same way about the other points as well where the world was ruled by pagan powers.

The new level of mutual love and forgiveness on which the redeemed community is called (and enabled by the Spirit) to live cannot be directly enforced on the larger society; but since it is the gospel, i.e., since it represents authentically good news for the real world, it will necessarily work as salt and light. This should be true anywhere; even more evidently should it be the case in the Anglo-Saxon world, where a large number of citizens claim some kind of Christian sanction for society's values. If Christ is not only prophet and priest but also king, the border between the church and the world cannot be impermeable to moral truth. Something of the cross-bearing, forgiving love, and dignity which Jesus' life, death, and resurrection revealed to be the normative way to be human, must be the norm for all humans, whether they know it or not. We cannot *expect* of anyone, not even of believers, that that norm be lived out perfectly. Yet, is the calling of the followers of Jesus to testify that there is no other norm. The one strategy which will not serve that calling, which could not be done in the first century, and cannot be done in our century, is to claim to possess, and to impose on society, a body of civil rules independent of the faith of the persons called to respect them. The alternative is to work within the acceptance of the others' unbelief, which is what I call "condoning" the lesser moral level of the civil order.

Some will claim that to challenge the death penalty in the name of Christ is to advocate anarchy. If sinners should be forgiven, if only the innocent may "throw the first stone," they ask, where will we stop? Does this not destroy all government?[4]

The question is not always meant sincerely. Most who ask it do not themselves propose to follow the Mosaic law by advocating capital punishment for adultery today. They do not really believe that society will collapse if rebellious sons are not executed by stoning. Nonetheless, the question does merit attention. It illustrates a real problem in relating Christian ethics to non-Christian society.

The first mistake that question makes is to assume that in interpreting a Christian social critique, the right question to ask is how to "carry things to their logical conclusion." That assumption distorts everything. Christian social criticism addresses a fallen world. Since that critique derives its ultimate standards from the kingdom of God—for there are no other *ultimate* standards—to "carry them to their logical conclusion" would mean the presence of that kingdom. Yet, that consistent application would demand faith. It lies beyond the capacities and the intentions of the rebellious world as it is in fact.

The Christian cannot expect that of fallen society. Thus to undercut Christ's call by asking "where would this lead?" is to distort the whole problem. By the fact of its rebellion, the "world" has guaranteed that Christian social critique will not lead "too far." Yet, the resurrection and ascension of Christ guarantee that there is no situation in which nothing can be done. The world can be challenged, one point at a time, to take one step in the right direction, to move up one modest notch in approximation of the righteousness of love.[5] To challenge capital punishment no more undermines government than does the rejection of the oath (Matt. 5:33–37, James 5:12) undermine truth-telling; no more than does the concept of the consent of the governed destroy the authority of the state.

The civil order is a fact. That it might be done away with by pushing the critique of love "too far" is inconceivable. We saw above that Genesis 9, like every primitive government, does not *demand* vengeance, since it is already present, but rather works to restrain it. Thus the Christian (and any believer in democracy) will be concerned to restrain the violent, vengeful potential of the state. That potential for violence does not need our advocacy; it is already there.

"Anarchy," the scare concept quoted above, is a grammatical abstraction, an intellectual construct, an imaginary entity. There is no such reality. There are varying forms of government, from tyranny to constitutional democracy; there are varying degrees of centralization of power, from the independent tribe through the "nation" to world empire. Where the criminal underground is highly organized, or in case of civil war, there may be two powers claiming authority over the same territory. There may be great variation in how effectively a power controls its subjects. Authority may be delegated or seized. It may be exercised wisely or wantonly, overtly or undercover, with or without a constitution, with or without the consent of the governed. But despite all these possible variations there *is* always authority.[6] In the (very rare) cases where it may seem that authority is functioning too little for the welfare and stability of society, the reason is never that the critique coming from the direction of Christian love has been too effective.

The scare concept of "anarchy" does not arise from the study of societies. It is the creature of the mental urge to carry things to their "logical conclusions"; an urge which is out of place in a fallen world.

The second error in the "where will we stop?" argument is the notion that there exists some clear and univocal concept of justice, having the same meaning in all times and places, consisting in an exact logical or mathematical equivalence of offense and retribution, and that such "justice" must (or can) be either wholly respected or fundamentally rejected. In real life—and in clear logic—there is no one sure yardstick by which to measure the "justness" of a penalty. Every culture and every age has different conceptions of what is fair retribution.[7] Opinions have changed enormously from culture to culture as to how much it matters whether the offender was human, adult, free and of a sound mind, and whether he was aware of the law he broke. They vary enormously as well in judging what "equivalent" means. "Eye for eye" is measurable if there has been bodily injury,[8] and "ox for ox" will work in case of material loss; but what are the equivalent penalties for adultery? for covetousness? We noted before that there is no command to lie to a liar or to rape a rapist.

Justice is a direction, not an achievement. It is a relative, not an absolute concept. Moral acts may be more just or less just, but we know of no ideal justice, distinct from love, which "too much emphasis on love" would jeopardize. Justice may well be undermined by lack of wisdom. It may be undermined by idealistic schemes for reformation, by social criticism which does not propose relevant alternatives, by a sentimental misunderstanding of the nature of love, or by failing to recognize to how great an extent order and mutual respect have already been achieved by the society one criticizes; but justice is not endangered by too much love.

THE DEATH PENALTY DEBATE

Despite Concessions, No Other Lord

The classical Christian confession referred to earlier states that Jesus is not only prophet, priest, and rabbi, but also Lord and King. Those are political names. Even the name "Christ" (the Anointed One) was originally a royal designation. Christians begin to deny their Lord when they admit that there are certain realms of life in which it would be inappropriate to bring Christ's rule to bear. Of course, non-Christians will insist that we should keep our *religion* out of the way of their *politics*. But the reason for that is not that Jesus has nothing to do with the public realm; it is that they want nothing to do with Jesus as Lord.

If we confess that it is the Lamb that was slain who is "worthy . . . to receive power and wealth and wisdom and might and honor and glory and blessing" (Rev. 5:12), we are relating the Cross to politics. If we ask who crucified Jesus and why, the Cross is political at the outset. What we believe about Christ must apply to all our behavior, no matter how many of our neighbors remain unconvinced. Of course, the unbelief and the contrasting beliefs of our neighbors, added to our own disobedience, will mean that no society will fully keep the law of God. When a society falls short of his law, God knows how to use even that disobedience for his glory. "Providence" is the traditional Christian word for the fact that God's being in charge of history includes his power sovereignly and savingly to take into account what the fallen world does against his will. This is not a reason for Christians to justify or to defend the lower level of behavior which results from unbelief, whether it be in the political realm or elsewhere.

The words of Paul in Romans 13:1–7, which affirm that the "powers that be" are subject to God, mean what I have just been saying. They have often been further interpreted to say that, since the powers are under God, therefore Christians have no grounds for criticizing what any given state does, or no standards to guide such a criticism. Paul does not say that. He says that government is "for our benefit" (v 4); that it is God's servant when (or insofar as) it "perseveres toward this very end" (v. 6).[9]

These expressions, as well as the parallel ones in 1 Peter 2:13ff, indicate that there are standards of good and right order, not dependent on the arbitrary judgment of individual rulers, by which government is to be judged. The state is not a law unto itself. This does not authorize

144

us to rebel against an unjust state by using against it the same weapons it uses oppressively. It does, however, give us standards for identifying oppression and grounds for denouncing it. No standard is more simply applicable to what governments do than "Thou shalt not kill."[10]

The Romans passage is but one application of a New Testament truth which is stated more frequently and more clearly in other texts. The broader claim is that "Christ is Lord" (Phil. 2:11; 1 Cor. 12:3). His status as "Lord" does not apply only to the church; Christ is exalted "far above every principality and power, and might, and dominion, and every name that is named . . ." (Eph. 1:21; Phil. 2:10; 1 Cor. 15:27; Matt. 28:18). Protestant tradition as we saw has used the term *providence* to say the same thing.

The world does not acknowledge Christ as Lord; but his being Lord is not dependent on the world's acknowledgement, any more than George Bush's being President in 1989 was dependent on whether all U.S. citizens and resident aliens liked him, or on whether they were all informed that he had been elected and inaugurated. A government, like any rebellious power, can attempt to be independent, can claim to be its own master, but Christians know that the claim is false and the attempt doomed to fail.

It is not our theme here to discuss the Christian view of government in general.[11] The mere confession of Christ's dominion generates conclusions sufficient for our present purpose. If it is as the apostles said, that Jesus Christ and not some other lord rules at the right hand of God over the powers of this world, then the purpose, goals, and standards of that rule can be no other than this same Jesus revealed to us, when in the flesh; he came not to destroy but to save. On the grounds of his rule, it can then not be the duty of governments to destroy life.

The Sword in Apostolic Thought

The New Testament Epistles are silent about capital punishment. The apostles do instruct their readers that they are to be subject to their rulers. Rulers are supposed to rule "for your benefit" (Rom. 13:4). Those who chose to break the law called down punishment upon themselves; but there is no reference in the epistles to specific penalties. Rulers should enable us to "lead religious and reverent lives in peace and quiet"

(1 Tim. 2:2). Governors should "punish criminals and encourage good citizenship" (1 Pet. 2:14), but there is no specification of the content either of the citizenship or the "punishment."

The "sword" (*machaira*), of which Paul writes to the Romans that rulers do not "bear it in vain," is the symbol of judicial authority, not the weapon of either war or the death penalty. In imperial Rome the *machaira* was not the arm either of the soldier in combat or of the executioner. The civil order as such is the theme of the passage. The state's taking of life is not.

There is in the Epistles no allusion to the provision for animal sacrifice or for killing killers in the covenant with Noah, and none of the apostles—Jews that they all were—would have thought of the Roman courts as applying the Mosaic penal provisions.

The Epistles say even less than do the Gospels about urging society to move toward the Kingdom; that should be no surprise. The Epistles are addressed to believers who constitute an infinitesimal minority within Roman/Mediterranean culture; there was no place for them to contemplate immediately effective social critique. The Gospels, on the other hand, recount Jesus' impact in a setting where Hebraic notions of divine justice were less alien. Jesus' gracious demands (or rather, offers) were not accepted by all who heard him, but they were not inconceivable for his Jewish hearers. The notions of a personal, caring, intervening, righteous, demanding, chastising God which underlay Jesus' message, and his forgiving practice, had been understandable to Jesus' Jewish hearers, but they would not have been to the polytheistic Romans.

It is thus formally wrong to look in the New Testament for specific guidelines for a good civil society. If such prescriptions had been given, they would embarrass us, as they would have had to be written to fit first-century Mediterranean conditions. We should rather look there for a general orientation toward ultimate human values and the nature of redemption, and then ask for our time what *those meanings* have to say. This is what happens when we remember that the foundational level of the Hebraic vision with which we began was not about civil penalties but about ritual expiation.

NOTES

1. The first narrative in chapter 8 is missing in some of the ancient manuscripts, and some doubt that it was originally part of the Gospel; but even those scholars who doubt that these verses were originally in John's Gospel tend to grant that it nonetheless represents an authentic tradition.

2. That the persons bearing the incriminating witness should cast the first stone is part of the provision of Deuteronomy 17:7.

3. Cf. p. 131,note 5, the reference to Bailey's exaggerated dislike for seeing moral meaning in narrative texts.

4. ". . . the opponents of capital punishment offer no theory of civil government..."; Gordon H. Clark, "Capital Punishment and the Bible," *Christianity Today*, February 1, 1960, p. 10. As a rationalistic philosopher, Clark felt that to have the right to say anything about human justice you must have a theory covering everything in the field.

5. Cf. my *Christian Witness to the State* (Newton, Kan.: Faith and Life Press, 1964), 60ff.

6. The above argument has to do with authority in the sense of the state. Sober social science will add that there are also always other kinds of non-state authority holding societies together; the orders of the clan, the marketplace, the school, religion, entertainment. . . .

7. See p. 207 on the variety of capital offenses in the Old Testament, and p. 113, note 154 on the variety of capital offenses in Anglo- Saxon legal tradition.

8. But cf. p. 133ff. where we note that in one of the three texts on "eye for eye" the offense to be punished "equally" was not wounding an eye but perjury about who had wounded an eye.

9. Cf. my *Politics of Jesus* (Grand Rapids: Eerdmans, 1972), pp. 207ff.

10. Jean Lasserre, "The 'Good' in Romans 13" in Donald Durnbaugh, ed., *On Earth Peace* (Elgin Ill.: Brethren Press, 1978), 130–35.

11. I do offer some of this in my *Christian Witness to the State*, (note 5 above), and in my *Priestly Kingdom* (Notre Dame, In.: Notre Dame University Press, 1985), 151–71.

5

Christ Transforming Culture

Among the differences between the biblical age and our own of which we must take account, there are the many new political institutions and cultural insights which have been developed, especially in recent centuries, particularly in our Anglo-Saxon world. We cannot study these matters here with the care they deserve, but to fail to name them would mean unconsciously making untested assumptions—favorable or unfavorable—about them. None of these developments is directly or uniquely Christian, but in general it could be shown that they have been derived—whether by a sequence of rational arguments or by historical experience—from the impact upon society of biblically-derived understandings.

1. Our culture has developed the notion of "rights" belonging to individuals by virtue of their being human, vested in each one by creation, not needing to be earned by some special performance or capable of being awarded only to a few as special privilege. This philosophical notion was stated at the foundation of our republic. Philosophically, this idea can be challenged. It is individualistic; just what all the "rights" are is hard to define in a way that convinces everyone. The people who first stated the theory did not believe that it applied to women or to people of other races.

Nonetheless, this notion of "rights" borne by each person is the best way we have yet found to interpret in our time, and to defend against encroachment by the authorities, the dignity of every person as created by God in his image. To say that every human being is endowed at birth with an inalienable right to life is our analogy to the Bible's speaking of the sacredness of blood. That that right is inalienable means that it cannot be transferred, even by the bearer himself. One cannot sell oneself into slavery; one cannot forfeit the right to live by misbehaving.

2. Constitutional democracy, in the special American form providing for an independent judiciary, freedom of speech, press, and assembly, habeas corpus, and the rights of due process (speedy and fair trial, the presumption of innocence, no self-incrimination), provides a wholesome way to discipline the innate tendency of the bearers of power to abuse the prerogatives of their office.[1] In some special circumstances, when due process rights serve to defend the accused, they are sometimes decried as "protecting criminals"; this is to forget that for the founding fathers of the U.S., as for the early Christians, and as for morally concerned persons in the nondemocratically governed majority of the world's societies even today, the primary threat to human dignity is not the impunity of individual offenders not proven guilty, but the absolute power to punish of the state itself.

Yet, because—in the Anglo-American system—the courts rather than the legislatures defend certain values, especially the rights of the accused, a regrettable arbitrariness is imposed on our society. If a case comes to the United States Supreme Court for review from Massachusetts or California it may enhance personal rights; if it comes from Georgia or Florida, it may not. The fact that government itself does not defend victims in general, to say nothing of the victims of wrongs done by the courts, has largely left significant social change to the initiative of tiny volunteer agencies which fight seemingly hopeless issues through the courts. Values won in the courts can be struck down again by legislatures, where demagoguery or the impact of a rare atrocity can sway votes more easily than fairness or compassion. Nonetheless, this system of checks and balances represents more adequately than does any modern alternative the biblical vision for a government which acknowledges its limits, and provides to its subjects the instruments whereby it may itself be held in line.

3. One large change which has gradually taken place during the last century and a half is consideration of the reduced accountability of the

very young and the mentally incompetent. Even the strong retentionist van den Haag does not call for reinstating death for children or the insane.[2] Certainly, this change is part of the long-range impact of Jewish and Christian humane sentiments, of a piece with the Mosaic provision of cities of refuge for the innocent or the demand for multiple witnesses.

4. All modern societies have seen over the past two centuries a striking diminution of use of the death penalty. Laws providing for death as the penalty for many crimes have been taken off the books.[3] Death sentences still possible in the law have been inflicted less frequently on those found guilty; they have more often been overruled on appeal. The quality of justice has been tempered with mercy *on the average*, even though the extent to which this has happened has been most uneven. As Chief Justice Wright of California wrote in 1972, even persons who want death penalty laws on the books apply them less and less:

> . . . among those persons called upon to actually impose or carry out the death penalty it is being repudiated with ever increasing frequency.
> . . . What our society does in actuality belies what it says [in the lawbooks] with regard to its acceptance of capital punishment.[4]

Wright is not describing here the work of "liberal" lobbies or public defenders, but that of the main line of prosecutors, juries, and courts of appeal. This growing humanization (Wright called it, quoting a 1958 Supreme Court decision, *Trop v. Dulles* "evolving standards of decency that mark the progress of a maturing society") is due, of course, to many factors within our society, but most of them are derived from the Hebraic and Christian value of compassion, the conviction that the sacredness of human life is a gift of God rather than something to be earned or easily forfeited, and the post-Christian sense of fairness which the democratic experience nurtures.

5. Most democratic societies tend over the years to grow in their recognition that discrimination based on race or class is unjust. Already two generations ago Warden Lewis E. Lawes of Sing Sing noted that no one was put to death who was not poor.[5] The system of public defenders for the indigent and the thin network of private-sector agencies which defend some individuals are still a far cry from fairness, but at

least our society at large recognizes the problem of unequal access to justice, and the courts will in some cases take account of it.

This kind of gradual "humanizing" change, however, is at the root of a new kind of injustice. The less frequently the maximum penalty is applied (as seen in the previous paragraph), the greater is the likelihood that the victims to whom it is still applied are chosen arbitrarily. It was this evident "capricious and arbitrary" unfairness that led to the 1972 Furman decision which struck down the extant death penalty laws until the laws were rewritten. To let live most persons found guilty of capital offenses and then to execute only a few, and to have those few chosen not on the grounds of the special nature of the crime but on the basis of their race, or of their means, or of the state in which they were tried, made those executions, it could be argued, into "cruel and unusual punishment," forbidden by the Eighth Amendment, or it identified them as "arbitrary and capricious," a denial of the "equal protection" provided by the Fourteenth Amendment.

6. The constitutional guarantees of the free exercise of religion and the prohibition of governmental action regarding "the establishment of religion" have been developed into the notion of "separation of church and state." The growing religious pluralism of our society makes it harder to connect faith-based moral convictions to public life. It opens complex debates about the framers' intent and how to read the Bill of Rights. The fathers of the Republic certainly did not intend to "establish" some kind of religious neutrality as preferable to religious commitment. That does leave a vacuum, or room for complex negotiation, among the religious perspectives which ought to count in public matters.

Some Protestant fundamentalists and some Roman Catholics deny that that "separation" can exempt the civil government from the jurisdiction of what they hold to be the revealed will of God, since the sacredness of human life, as distinct from some other social values, is a matter of natural moral law, not of denominational diversity. This is not a matter concerning *directly* only the death penalty; its most immediate contested relevance in practical politics today is, in fact, is to the abortion debate. Yet, *if taken consistently*, this argument would have to apply as well to the death penalty. For American Catholics today, it does apply against the death penalty, as quite parallel to the wrongness of abortion. For some fundamentalists, on the other hand, it may apply in favor of capital punishment, although not many "right to life" advocates have argued openly, as logically it would seem they should have to, that death should be the penalty for abortion. Conflicts of that kind, between people who agree that "nature" or "the law of God" teaches just one thing, regardless of denomination, weakens logically their claim that the natural moral law is evident to everyone. If it really were evident to all, there would be no argument. That should invite to greater modesty anyone making the claim to interpret revelation with final authority. It tends to mean that when Christians converse with their fellow citizens in the public arena, they properly should express their values in terms the neighbors can follow. Thus, it does not count against the Christian opponent of the death penalty that others—"liberals", humanists, Jews—may support the sacredness of life in terms other than references to Creation and Cross, which are most clear for the Christian, and which I have been using here.

Let us look back at these developments taken all together; we may speak of them as cultural transformation under the pressure of the gospel, or as humanization. Some socially conservative Christians, for reasons which they have not yet thought through carefully, have come to speak as if "humanism" were opposed to Christian commitment. It is true that there are ways, as there are a few people choosing those ways, to seek to separate the value of the "human" from God's concern as Creator and Redeemer. True: one can be "humanist" in an atheistic or "secularistic" frame of reference.

Yet we must refuse to concede "ownership" of the "human" to those who deny creation and redemption. The God of creation, making mankind in his image, was the first humanist. The story of the "humanization" of Western culture—limping, imperfect as it is, but real—is part of the work of the God of Abraham, Father of Jesus, partly done through his body, the church. That humanization of cultures is not the same as the salvation of individual souls, nor is it the same as the praise of God in gatherings for worship, nor is it the same as the coming of the ultimate Kingdom of God, but it is a fruit of the gospel for which we should be grateful, and for whose furtherance we are responsible. The fact that persons believing in other value systems share in the humanization process, and that some of them may overvalue it, as if it could do away with evil, is no reason for followers of Jesus to disavow it, or to leave it to unbelievers to carry out.[6]

NOTES

1. The phrasing above is not legally precise or exhaustive. Some of these values are defined or safeguarded in particular articles of the Bill of Rights, some by custom, some by statute.

2. Van den Haag does argue, as I would, that insanity would best be considered as a factor in determining proper punishment, rather than as ground for a "not guilty" finding.

3. There were over 220 capital crimes in England around 1800; cf. Koestler, 7.

4. *People* [California] versus *Anderson*, 1972.

5. We have cited Warden Lawes more than once. It is noteworthy that several highly respected professionals in corrections have come to reject the death penalty *in the name of* their concern for the effective implementation of the laws; Clinton Duffy of Alcatraz and Lawrence Wilson of San Quentin. Wilson reported that most wardens agree with him against the death penalty: p. 123 in Gray and Stanley (see bibliography).

6. Cf. p. 108, 153, and 175, my recognition that numerous "humane" or "liberal" arguments, which this study does not survey, are nonetheless valid.

6

The Clash of Rationales

We began in the middle of the debate; our attention has ranged thus far across some of the main themes in biblical backgrounds. We have tested the assumptions of those who *assumed* their views to be biblically founded. We have looked at how Christian concern moves on from biblical times to our own. We can now proceed toward a sort of synthesis of the state of the question.

That offenses must be punished, all societies agree. Yet why this should be is not agreed. A great variety of reasons are given for punishment. Even when the same words are used, the meanings differ. Several of the texts in our bibliography have sought to spread these reasons out along a logical spectrum. Gerber and McAnany, for instance, list four: retribution, rehabilitation, deterrence, and "social defense." Conrad lists the same four but calls them retribution, reform, intimidation, and incapacitation.

This possibility of a neat listing may give the first impression that the debate is more orderly than it is. Ernest van den Haag, one of the shrewdest debaters, denies that "retribution" standing alone is a meaningful concept, but thinks that "justice" is. What he means by "justice" is after all what others call "retribution." In any case, we must seek to make some kind of order, in the awareness that word usage varies:

1. Retribution is the first category of justification we now must turn to interpreting. A careful observer must distinguish within the realm of

"retribution" at least three quite different strands of justification for doing evil for evil:

A. The victim of any crime, or in the case of murder the next of kin and the neighbors, may desire emotionally that there be pain inflicted on the guilty person. The simplest and more accurate name for this is "revenge." The sentiment which demands it is anger. Van den Haag calls it "an emotion universally felt . . . which all societies must gratify." Yet certainly there are deeply and widely felt emotions which should not be gratified. Racism and xenophobia are deeply and widely felt emotions too. The near-universal experience of history, as van den Haag (p. 13) also recounts, until recent centuries called as well for elaborate torture, making immediate death a form of mercy. Today, however, we do not gratify legally that appetite, and van den Haag does not suggest that we should.

B. It may be held that God (B/1), or the gods (B/2), or "the moral order" (B/3), demands retribution. The classical image is that of a balance, where evil done on one side can be compensated for by pain inflicted on the other. Yet, why a second wrong should right the first one is not easily explained. It cannot count as a universal moral demand without more argument.

C. It may be held that the dignity of the offender himself demands that he should pay the price of his offense. Part of being human is taking responsibility for the results of one's actions. To be adult in the economy is to be able to make promises and to be held to keeping them. The same should apply to paying the price of one's offenses. Sometimes (C/1) it is society which tells the offender that his taking his "deserved" punishment is the price of his readmission into society. Sometimes (C/2) it is the individual who, one argues, knows his guilt and wants to pay for it. C. S. Lewis, the well-known Anglican apologist of mid-century, argued strongly for the notion of deserved punishment as a part of the human dignity of the offender, over against "humanistic" notions of punishment as rehabilitation (3. below), or of excusing the crime as socially caused.[1]

Some criminals do want to be executed. Some psychotherapeutic theories see "guilt" as the person's having so thoroughly internalized the value system of the surrounding power structure as to want to be punished. But the fact that the offender thinks he should be killed does not prove that he should.

Which of these three—in fact, at least five or six—different arguments is the "real" meaning of retribution? Our point is precisely that there is no right answer to that question; the debate is far more complex. To boil them all down to one or the other is to be deceived and to deceive. Beneath them, i.e., deeper in cultural history, there are yet two other levels, somewhat like B. above (God or the gods) yet not the same.

D. The literal sense of Genesis 9:6, when taken alone, does not refer to crime in general, or to moral offenses against God's commands, but specifically and only to the shedding of blood. It does not cover the *lex talionis* as a general rule for retribution or the penal provisions of the Mosaic laws. In the covenant with Noah, a sacrificial view of our link to the animal world and to God as its Creator makes killing a sacrilege. The blood which is the life belongs to God its giver; the killer forfeits his life by that act of desecration. "Retribution" is a possible term here, but "expiation" might be more adequate. Its frame of reference is the sacral cosmos, not the social contract. The "balance" it restores is cosmic and ceremonial, not moral or legal.

E. According to René Girard, literary critic turned cultural anthropologist, the reality which underlies both B. and D. above is a prehistoric cultural transaction, an event whereby the primitive vengefulness which sufficed to maintain order in prehistoric societies was replaced by killing a substitute. In order for this primeval, vicarious, ritual killing to "work," i.e., to have the effect of pacifying society, its meaning must be covered over with the cultural artifice of myth and poetry. It can be unearthed only, as Girard has done it, by dint of careful archaeological and anthropological sleuthing. To interpret and evaluate Girard's hypothesis would take us much too far[2]: yet he represents the most serious effort in contemporary cultural studies to make sense of a basic social fact: namely, the way in which society's viability is thought to demand that the quasi-universal appetite for violent retaliation must be at the same time both validated and buffered, both satisfied and diverted, both acknowledged and denied.

2. Under the heading "incapacitation," "prevention," or "social defense" we find the varieties of justification given for incarceration as well as for execution. The action is based not on "setting right" a past offense but on preventing what one holds is a likely future one. Certainly there are

offenders who if freed might offend again, although the recidivism rate for persons who have killed is less than for other crimes. It is doubtful that this justification calls for killing someone who has already been made harmless by incarceration. Many who have killed in the past will not do so again. This consideration would call for discrimination on the basis not of past guilt but of future prospects.

3. Under "rehabilitation" or "reform" we find those views which would make incarceration a positive service to the offender by helping him or her become a better person. Some prisons have been called "reformatories" or "penitentiaries" with this understanding. Society has a right to demand that people become good before setting them free. For some, this is a subcategory of the "social defense" notion; for others, it expresses a more optimistic view of human nature. We have noted C. S. Lewis's claim that it insults the personal dignity of the offender to manipulate his character and condition his liberties by criteria other than desert. Lewis links this mentality with another issue, namely his polemic against the "liberal" idea that people are not to blame for their crimes, or should not be called to retribution, because of their lack of opportunity, lack of good parental models, or other exonerating considerations.[3] So this category, too, is complex rather than univocal; yet *for our purposes* this is not very important, since this is the one of the four standard reasons, applicable to punishments in general, which can never be used to justify the death penalty.

4. There remains deterrence, or intimidation, with which we began. The arguments against it were surveyed before (see p. 113ff.); as we have gone along it has become increasingly evident that the generally assumed equation of deterrence with the Mosaic or the "cosmic order" warrants for retribution is incorrect.

Which View Is Right?

In the face of such a complex spectrum of views, our normal intellectual defense mechanism is to oversimplify and to excommunicate. We would like to be told why one view is clearly right and to overrule the others. Yet, the discussion rules of a free society will not permit that, nor will the gospel. The several modes are all socially operative. They are all part of the discussion, whether we deem them worthy or not. The most powerful are sometimes the least morally worthy (e.g., vengeance) or the most tied to a bygone worldview (the retaliatory world order, where a second wrong makes a right). What we here properly should retain, both from the Old Testament and from the universal presence of retribution in human societies, is not one right general theory about the background "reasons" for the death penalty, but the fact of its universality. The various "reasons" are all relevant, all meaningful to someone, and all questionable when examined morally more closely.

Our interest should rather be to discern, *in the midst* of this complexity, what the Christian gospel has to say. We have already seen that the constant theme of the Hebrew story is God's intervening to save the guilty. This begins by his saving Cain, the prototypical murderer, from the lethal workings of the talion. It continued in the covenant with Noah in that, although letting stand the concept of blood vengeance, God held it in the setting of sacrifice, parallel to God's jealous ownership of the blood of every victim, and not authorizing the escalation threatened by Lamech. It continued in the age of national Israel, in that although legislation obtained broadly like that of the neighboring peoples, its harshness was mitigated. There was no indirect talion, there were refuges for the accidental killer (at the places of worship, continuing the sacral connection of Genesis 9), and more than one witness was needed to condemn.[4]

The Bible's witness on these matters is a long story, not a timeless, unchanging corpus of laws or of truths. What matters for us is not the cultural substance of where the story started (with its racism, its superstition, its slavery, its holy warfare, its polygamy, and its abuse of women), but where it was being led. That direction is toward Jesus; toward validating the dignity of every underdog and outsider, of the slave and foreigner, the woman and the child, the poor and the offender. This is done not on the grounds that this or that outsider is an especially virtuous person, but on the grounds of God's grace.

The culmination of the story for our purposes is that the Cross of Christ puts an end to sacrifice for sin. The sacrificial worldview of Genesis 9 is not abandoned by the New Testament as culturally obsolete, as we are tempted to do. It is rather assumed and fulfilled, when the Epistle to the Hebrews takes as its central theme the way the death of Christ is the end of all sacrifice. The most primitive, the culturally most basic rootage of violence against the violent is freely faced and nonviolently accepted by Jesus the innocent, reluctant, but ultimately willing victim of an unjust execution.[5]

> The love of Christ leaves us no choice,
> when once we have reached the conclusion
> that one man has died for all
> and therefore all mankind has died. (2 Cor. 5:14, NEB)

To say it in the most orthodox theological terms, the end of expiation for bloodshed, the end—not as abrogation but as fulfillment—of the arrangement announced in Genesis 9:6, is the innocent death of the Son, wrongly denounced by a righteous religious establishment and wrongfully executed by a legitimate government.

By unjustly condemning the Righteous One in the name of the Pax Romana and the welfare of the people (John 11:50, 18:14) the claimants to human righteousness refuted their claim for the rightness of the death penalty in the very act of imposing it.

That is the specifically Christian way to say it—although as Gandhi and Girard show us, one need not be Christian to see it. The power bearers of this world will not understand it in these terms, so we shall need to find ways to translate. We may speak of the unity of all humanity under the indiscriminate providence of God; of inalienable rights endowed by the Creator, of crime being partly the result of a bad social situation, of the right to life being inalienable, and therefore not something which a person can lose by doing evil.

All of these translations or parables are inadequate. Yet they are all valid parts of the argument in a multicultural democracy. They are not true in themselves as secular philosophical dicta, but for what they point to, namely, to the grand reversal of world history when the Maker and Model became willingly the victim, bearing all human retribution, whether merited or not, dying the death earned not only by the murderer but by all of us.

NOTES

1. Lewis's special concern (see bibliography) was that if some social elite takes over deciding what makes us worthy of returning to society independently of considerations of just desert, that could become tyrannical. He had been provoked to write this test by the British debate about capital punishment. Yet he did not stretch his argument to the claim that every killer's human dignity does or should make him want to die.

2. I offered a very brief resume of Girard's thought in *Religion and Literature* 19/3, Autumn 1987, 89–92. The importance of Girard for Christian thinking about atonement and capital punishment is summarized by Raymund Schwager, *Must There Be Scapegoats?* (San Francisco: Harper and Row, 1986)

3. It is not clear whether Lewis would on these grounds oppose all exonerating arguments based on insanity, retardation, or duress. He would accept exonerating children, which already weakens the rigor of his case.

4. Bailey, 27–31, lists further ways in which the general retributive drive was mitigated.

5. Oddly yet profoundly, René Girard makes the same point in the terms of his new synthesis of cultural anthropology and literary history. He affirms the

7

The Test of Consistency

This is not the first time in the course of our pilgrimage through our problem that I have needed to show how the public debate about legal death has become clouded, so that what I most need to argue is not whether life, even guilty life, is sacred but rather the inconsistencies of the case usually made for the death penalty.

Do You Really Mean It?

Probably the most strongly believed claim of those who advocate the retention of the supreme sanction is that the death penalty as currently practical is the same as what God once commanded—whether in the very broad terms of the covenant given Noah or in the more detailed legislation given Moses. This claim does not constitute a rational argument, but it is the conviction held to the most self-confidently by those who are most sure that their views are biblically warranted.

It is that unquestioning self-confidence which we here must proceed to test, approaching so to speak "from the inside." We shall bring to light the fact that people who think this is what they believe are not in fact consistent. Most of those who *claim* to be using the ancient biblical argument in favor of the death penalty have not faced the challenge of what it would mean to apply it consistently. There is no evidence—

163

even in the most strongly argued books on the subject—that the costs of such consistency have been weighed. There is a great distance between saying "the death penalty cannot be wrong because the Bible commands it" and saying "the death penalty laws of my state and nation are what God commands." For example:

- Most persons found guilty of capital crimes by our courts are not sentenced to death, but to some lesser punishment. Christians authentically taking Genesis 9:6 literally as the last word of God would have to be aggressively active in getting all of those sentences made harsher, not only in those cases where the murder was particularly atrocious.
- Many persons sentenced to death are not executed after all. A rare few are still alive to be released when new evidence shows them to have been innocent. Some make deals with the prosecution, some benefit from executive clemency, some are saved on appeal because of procedural errors made by police or prosecutors, some die or are killed in prison. . . . Christians concerned to defend Genesis 9:6 as legislation would have to be especially concerned for saving those in the first category and for assuring the execution of all the others.
- The Mosaic legislation in general made (as we observed) no reference to mitigating considerations and no provision for lack of premeditation. For every death in an automobile accident or in medical malpractice someone should die. Insanity should be no defense, nor youth. In the conservative Christian literature arguing in favor of the death penalty, one finds little precision about whether these defenses or mitigating pleas should be swept away or respected.
- Those who claim divine revelation as ground for modern jurisprudence are not usually clear about *which* revelation they mean. The laws of Moses (cf. p. 207, and Bailey, pp. 17–22) are clear in demanding death for rebellious adolescents, for a bride's deceiving her husband concerning her virginity, for adultery, for sabbath-breaking, for homosexuality, and for false prophecy. If this *is* truly what our pro-death contemporaries mean, they should say so, and somehow deal honestly with the fact that in the U.S. in

particular the direct application of provisions from the Scriptures of one religious community would constitute the establishment of (one particular) religion, contrary to the First Amendment. Do they mean to obtain this legislation through democratic due process? If democratic due process does not work, will they take the law into their own hands?

If, on the other hand, what they mean to appeal to in favor of the death penalty is not the entire Mosaic Law, and if they mean to speak only of death as the penalty for murder, in line with Genesis 9:6, that would be intellectually understandable, on the ground that the covenant with Noah applies to all humanity, as the laws of Moses do not. Yet, it would be a very different claim, since that Genesis report on God's words to Noah is not a legislative text. Most of the capital provisions of the books of Moses would have to be dropped. The very point of the word to Noah is that *only* murder is ground for bloodshed in return.

When I point out that my fellow Christians who *think* they are in favor of retaining death penalty laws on biblical grounds are, in fact, inconsistent, my concern is not that they ought to become more consistent by working for a much more lethal government. Consistency is not a virtue if it applies to the hilt an inadequate rule or insight. Inconsistency is not a sin but it may be a flag, a marker indicating the possibility of self-deception or self-contradiction; it signals that one may not be doing what one does for the reason immediately avowed.

My concern is rather that those who have been led to think that the retentionist stance is obviously Christian should recognize that what they really want is not more killing after all. What they really want is compassion for the victims of crime, or security in an increasingly violent society, or a dramatic statement about the sanctity of life, or reassurance that the values of their faith have some standing in society. I want those things too; but asking our civil order to be more bloodthirsty is not the way to work toward them. These fellow citizens *have been led to believe* that that is what God has called for, and that more vengeful laws would provide that; but they do not really deeply believe that. If they did, there would have to be a pro-death counterpart of the American Civil Liberties Union, dedicated to increasing a thousandfold the number of offenders our society legally kills.

As a matter of fact, however, ("fact" both in verifiable social experience and in facing all the issues in rational argument), those same goals—compassion for victims, security, affirming the sanctity of *all* life, addressing public values from a faith stance—would be better served by a thorough antideath witness, continuing the "humanization" process in which Christians have been leading for centuries.

8

When the Death Penalty Itself Is Murder

The previous point at which the advocates of retention needed to be challenged was their conviction—more an assumption taken for granted than an argument they would recognize the need to support—that the modern legal practice of capital punishment is in some important way like the biblical precedents they claim.

Now we move to another dimension of our challenge to the integrity of the retentionist tradition; namely, its failure to avow the fallibility of human instruments of justice, and therefore its failure to recognize that in a small but real percentage of cases the innocent are killed *by the state, in our name,* in the defense of our society's power system.

All human institutions are fallible. They are capable of errors of fact or of interpretation. According to Christian convictions, all humans are sinful, using power, including sometimes the power of the law, for purposes less than purely honest and unselfish.

One of the great values of the democratic vision of civil government is its realism about human fallibility. If a tyrant were perfectly wise and good, tyranny would be the most efficient form of government. We need freedom of speech and assembly and the press, we need constitutions, guaranteed rights of majorities and individuals, elections, checks and balances, to keep under control the real possibilities of error and of misused authority.

In the courts this kind of corrective control is exercised by higher courts through the right of appeal. But there is one kind of judicial error that can never be made right: a wrongful sentence of death. The death penalty assumes that the judicial process is infallible and has all the evidence; yet we do not assume infallibility and omniscience in any other branch of government.

Lafayette is credited with saying: "Until the infallibility of human judgment shall have been proved to me, I shall demand the abolition of the penalty of death." His friend Thomas Jefferson is quoted as saying practically the same thing. No matter who said it first; should not persons seeking a biblically oriented view of things have even more profound reasons than the noble French general or the deist Federalist had, to believe both in the sacredness of every human life and in the fallibility of every human institution?

Christian sobriety calls us to mistrust any social practice whose mistakes are irrevocable. Even the lesser penalties of unjust incarceration are irrevocable, in that the years they steal from a person's life cannot be returned. It is one of the institutionalized injustices of our society that in most jurisdictions there is no standard provision for compensation to those subjected wrongfully to lesser penalties of conviction and punishment.[1] Yet death imposed on an innocent person is the absolutely incorrigible error. It is murder, committed in the name of the people.

The works of Borchard, Frank, Stanford, and Bedau in our bibliography detail some *known* cases of the innocent being convicted.[2] There are scores of them. They happen because of (innocently or malevolently) false testimony, mistaken identity, or misinterpreted circumstantial evidence. By the nature of the case it is a matter of chance that these particular examples have come to light.[3]

Likewise, by the nature of the case it is seldom possible or useful to review such a case judicially after execution. The American legal system has no agency responsible for keeping track of miscarriages of justice. When such errors come to light it is through the disinterested curiosity of some journalist, the persistent pleading of the victim's family, or a later confession by the really guilty person. There must be more cases than we can know, in which no one brought forward the facts that would have exonerated the accused. The famous warden Lewis Lawes of Sing Sing spoke for his colleagues in estimating that one in fifty of the persons executed by the state is innocent. Others estimate 5 percent.

Retentionists can continue to argue that the danger of such miscarriages of justice is slight, though the testimony of those who monitor current penal practice is not reassuring. But the Christian attitude should not be to quibble about whether the rate of judicially sanctioned murders is 5 percent or 2 percent. That such killings can occur *at all* is the question. A *fallible* civil order should never lay claim to *absolute* authority over life. It should *in the name of its own honor* deny itself the right to make irrevocable decisions.[4] The courts should do the best they can, without interrupting the normal course of justice out of the fear of making mistakes;[5] but this can be done confidently only if the door is left open for review and for new evidence.

The point at which we began to consider the need for Christian sobriety about the fallibility of social institutions was the jeopardy of the innocent; yet there are other instances as well of sinfulness in the system. Our courts are routinely discriminatory in terms of race and class. Despite the theoretical right of all to counsel, only the wealthy (and a few individuals whose peculiarly promising cases are taken on by voluntary agencies) are assured adequate legal assistance. Especially in Texas, Louisiana, and Florida, where executions are the most numerous, a Caucasian convicted of the same crime will not receive the same sentence as a black, the same crime committed against a Caucasian will be punished more harshly than against a black, and in proportion to the number of crimes committed the Caucasian will be less likely to be convicted.[6] Any retentionist claiming to be motivated, not by fear or vengeance, but by the honor of an impartially gracious God would have to be actively militating against these injustices.

The fact that execution closes and locks a door which morally should be kept open has numerous other undesirable accessory effects upon the administration of justice, beyond the obvious evil of making an error of a court irreparable. The prosecution of murder cases in states with the death penalty is much more slow, and is a greater burden on the courts and on the taxpayers, because the defense will leave no stone unturned, no costly appeal untried. One case in California took over ten years and cost the state over half a million dollars. Abolition states need not maintain a separate death row.

Penologists tell us in addition that the very presence of the death penalty on the books is a symbolic block, preventing direct attention

169

to the other unsolved problems of prison administration and reform. Overcrowding of prisons, education, recreation, work and rehabilitation, procedures of parole and resocialization, are catastrophically in need of new measures. To take the death penalty off the books will solve none of them. In terms of human pain, lifetime incarceration without prison reform might be, in fact, a fate as unpleasant as death. Yet the cultural defensiveness and vengefulness which keep the absolute sanction on the books are barriers to their being addressed adequately. The retention of the gas chamber, the gallows, and the chair, enshrining as they do the retributive mentality and the state's claim to absolute competence, warp our view of all the other problems. Prisons in other countries are ahead of those in the U.S. in the humaneness of their living conditions and their effectiveness in rehabilitation; some think that our entire corrections enterprise is vitiated by the notion of vengeance as the underlying goal of the system, of which capital punishment is the extreme symbol even when seldom inflicted. Its abolition in the other Western democracies symbolically undermines that barrier to creativity.

Some Christians have argued that to speak of the treatment of criminals in terms of therapy and rehabilitation rather than punishment, as "liberal" or "humanistic" penologists do, would be to deny the moral nature of the offense, or to excuse guilt as only an illness. This is not the point. The issue is not whether there is moral guilt; of course there is.[7] The issue is what the Christian attitude to the guilty should be. If our priority social preoccupation is with defending an abstract moral order by means of punishment, rather than with the redemption of persons, public offenders will, of course, continue to be the most accessible victims of our self-righteousness.

NOTES

1. Block, p. 1. Sometimes a state legislature will make some amends for wrongful incarceration by a private law, if there is a public outcry, but our legal system does not acknowledge a *right* to compensation for miscarriages of justice.

2. Borchard (see bibliography), 374f, 415ff; cf. also Charles Black.

3. Cf. "Miscarriages of Justice and the Death Penalty" in Bedau, 1983, 234ff.

4. "It belongs to its nature as an orderly society that its measures can have only a provisional, relative and limited character, that they must always be in a position to be transcended and corrected. But in punishing by death it does

170

something unlimited, irrevocable and irreparable." Karl Barth (see bibliography), 444.

5. We honor the fact that in our society certain due process rights are respected. The defense of constitutional rights in the U.S. Supreme Court suspended executions for a while in the 1970s, and has made some kinds of convictions more complicated. These rights make the prosecution of capital cases through the various levels of appeal enormously time-consuming and expensive. Prosecutions costing the government over half a million dollars are not rare. If the accused is wealthy, there is practically no end to the possible delays. Removing capital punishment would greatly alleviate the burdens on some courts.

6. The evidence of this bias has been recognized by the courts, and the growing complexity of the sentencing process takes some account of it. (Cf. the Meltzner account of the backgrounds to Furman.) Yet, the courts are a weak remedy for a deep injustice in our culture, especially when the moral elites appealing to the courts do not have strength at the polls. The effect of the corrective measures partly achieved through the events in the 1970s has begun to be largely eroded both by new legislation and by the rulings of the Reagan Supreme Court.

7. Cf. George N. Boyd, "Capital Punishment: Deserved and Wrong," *Christian Century*, February 17, 1988, 162–65.

9

From Survey to Synthesis: Denying the Legitimacy of the Death Penalty

Thus far I have been faithful to the initially stated method. I have responded to one issue at a time, from the middle of the current social debate, picking up the themes and slogans which already dominate that debate. This has meant questioning some of the simplest and least self-critical assumptions of those who hitherto have carried on the discussion on both sides.

I have not repeated the naive claim that "thou shalt not kill" in the Decalog is a direct prohibition of judicial killing. That argument is made, too simply, by some of those who call for the death penalty to be abolished or radically restricted. The meaning of "thou shalt not kill" certainly did not, in the original setting, literally exclude all killing, since the Ten Words stand side by side in the Mosaic texts with others which provide for legal killing.

That does not, however, justify the simple way some declare this text irrelevant, by saying that it means merely "do not murder." Logically, the distinction between "murder" and other killing is not that clear. Our society's laws distinguish a number of different degrees of murder and culpable manslaughter. The Hebrew language has a number of different words for taking human life, but the usage in the Hebrew is too infrequent to permit saying that *rsh* (also spelled *ratsach*), the Hebrew verb in the Sixth Commandment, means only "murder" in some narrow modern sense. It can include killing in legal retribution (Num. 35:27). Several respected recent Hebrew scholars have suggested that the original meaning was "do not take the law into your own hands."[1] Then this wording in the Decalog would testify to the transition from the primitive form to which Genesis 4 and 9 testify, with the "blood avenger" (cf. p. 122) being the next of kin, to the jurisdiction of some tribunal (such as the "judges" of the time before Saul, or the "elders in the gates" of an Israelite town). It would then in its original import have been a measure of restraint, a check on the arbitrariness and escalation which marked that primitive arrangement.

Thus without being literalistic about "thou shalt not kill," we should still with confidence affirm that the sacredness of human life is rooted in the Law. We do not relativize the call to sexual integrity with the argument that for the ancient Hebrews "thou shalt not commit adultery" did not forbid polygamy, harem slavery, and concubinage. We do not relativize "do not give false witness" by limiting it to lying before a court of law. In Christian moral instruction we give an extensive, not a minimalist, reading to the other commands of the Decalog.

We may now be in a position to state, with more care and clarity than would have been possible at the outset, how we then *should* take the total witness of the Scripture story, including the place of legal killing in the Hebrew heritage. That legislation cannot be taken as a simple institutional imperative—timeless, placeless, demanded by God of all societies regardless of culture or creed. The Hebrew Bible is not and does not claim to be that kind of civil law. If there was a time and place where some of those texts applied as civil law, it would *at most* have been thinkable between the time of Joshua and that of Josiah. Nothing in the teaching of the prophets, or the later rabbis, or the New Testament, indicates that ancient Israelite civil legislation, with its score of capital offenses, was meant to be universal. It was abandoned in the sixth century B.C., together with Israelite statehood, not only by the Jews but by God, even in its own land.

Before there were those civil rules, there was the different witness of Genesis, in the previous covenant, the one with Noah. As we saw, there exists only one occasion for shedding blood, namely prior bloodshed. The rootage for this was not a practical view of protecting the civil order but a sacral view of restoring the cosmic order. This demand for mimetic vengeance was present before history began (Gen. 4); God's first action was to limit it, whereas Cain's lineage escalated it. Even less than can obtain for the case rules of Exodus through Deuteronomy, we have no way to make the Genesis 9 arrangement a basis for civil law. Our American practice of capital punishment at its most rigorous falls far short of expiating every death with another death.

How then should we take this Hebrew heritage? Many Jews, Christians, and other contemporaries take for granted that it is obsolete, irrelevant, and that we should build our society on newer insights. Then they have numerous other good reasons, reasonable in our time, to oppose capital punishment. Most of those "other good reasons" are, in fact, very strong, although I have not made much of them:

- the general dehumanizing effect it has on a society to assume that it is up to us to dispose of human life;
- the general humane vision according to which every human life, even the unwanted and the morally unworthy, is sacred. Persons who abandon the details of ancient Israelite social norms still understand the notion of the divine image in every person;
- modesty about the inaccuracy and fallibility of human power structures; without making a statement about the value of any particular individual's life, a low view of government's righteousness will militate against granting that government absolute sovereignty over life and death;
- sobriety about how the presence of the death penalty on the books makes all the administration of justice slower, costlier, and less fair;
- sobriety about the number of innocent individuals statistically sure to be killed due to the fallibility of the police and the courts;
- a psychological understanding according to which anger and revenge are drives unworthy of mature persons and destructive to social civility.

These arguments are strong; they suffice for most citizens who think about it at all carefully to decide, on general humane grounds, in favor of the general trend of recent centuries in the West away from the use of death as a civil penalty. For our present assignment, however, they do not suffice to set aside what is really present, both in the Hebrew Scriptures and in popular culture, by way of demand for retaliation.

This demand for retribution may be called "vengeance," "expiation," "mimesis," or something else, depending on the fine-tuning of your social science; but it is always there. It is still there in the strongest prodeath arguments, those of Berns and van den Haag (see bibliography). These two contemporary authors most openly renounce arguing from any specified critical moral or philosophical commitment of their own (except for showing the weakness of others' too simple reliance on rehabilitation models). They argue only from the brute fact of vengeful anger as a universal (and, they believe, salutary) human phenomenon.[2] Neither Berns nor van den Haag follows his argument to its logical conclusions, which in historical perspective until very recently called for torturing offenders before killing them, or for including in the scope of vengeance the offender's family members. Berns does not even ask that all killers be killed—only the most vile (p. 183). Thus, they too have been somewhat swept up in the general influence of Jewish and Christian humanism since the Renaissance. They affirm retribution as a political imperative in the worst cases, not as a moral imperative in all cases.

That deep demand for death as redemption for death will not go away under the criticism of modern reasonableness.[3] But neither would a world be livable in which it would have the last word. Since Yahweh's intervention in Genesis 4, it is no longer the last word; another story has begun. It is the story of restraint, of sacrifice to defend and restore the cosmic order. That story comes to its first culmination in the Cross of Christ, in which utter innocence died for universal guilt, satisfying and thereby putting to an end the mechanisms of mimetic vengeance.[4] From then on the story that is needed is ours. Christ's followers, for whom his Cross has ended all sacrifice for sin, are to be, if we believe in him as the last word, the instruments of the pardon and the new style of response to evil which he enabled and enjoined.

Love of enemy is the gospel theme where the linkage between Christ himself and the believer's stance and calling in the world is closest. Forgiveness is the response to evil dictated by God's own nature and by Jesus' example and command.[5] We should seek to save the life even of the murderer fully culpable of the act for which society wants to kill him. The death penalty is wrong, not because it is not merited by some, but because merit is not the basis on which, since Jesus, we should decide who has a right to belong to the human race.

If the Bible were to be read fundamentally as a source of timeless, changeless rules for civil societies, it would document God's failure, since the narrative moved farther and farther from any such vision of a stable national theocracy, ever since the death of Solomon. If, on the other hand, the Bible is the story of God's unceasing interventions to move humankind in the direction of righteousness and well-being, then we must read the early chapters of Genesis as the point of departure of that story, rather than as definitive legislation. We can likewise read the documents of the early Israelite nation as a beginning movement, from which the unfolding, which did in fact happen, properly needed to happen, away from death as sanction threatened for a score of offenses (we do not know how long or how consistently any of these rules was in fact enforced), toward a society which can live at peace without having to kill anyone.

God's identity, i.e., God's being authentically and faithfully Who God is, and not something or somebody else, does not consist in timelessness resisting all change, so that his first word in Genesis would be also his last. His identity consists in his moving and working always in the same direction, through all of these centuries. That "same direction" we know best, most clearly in Jesus, but when we avow that fact, then in its light we can understand the ancient Israelite events and documents as already constituting part of that work, moving in that direction.

We have read, with more care than is usual, the Old Testament passages, which some think demand the civil penalty of death, and it has regularly come to light that they do not mean that. We have learned to discern with more care the difference between civil law, affirmations of a sacred cosmic order, and other ways of knowing about God's will. Each in its place, when read in the way that belongs to its kind and style of language, shows God at work, moving in the same way toward what Jesus ultimately did, toward ending blood vengeance by sacrificing himself.

It is that movement, broadening over the centuries into the derived forms of democracy, humanism, habeas corpus and the other rights of the accused, which since Beccaria has spread out into nonreligious parallels, and which in our day seeks—not yet very successfully—positive responses to the offender which will link respect for his human dignity with the protection of the innocent and restoration for victims.

The standard accounts in the literature, which I have played back in the notes in the bibliography, indicate that challenges to the death penalty began to be raised in western Europe in the eighteenth century, with the secular legal philosopher Beccaria and the Philadelphia physician Benjamin Rush (see bibliography). That is however inaccurate; it was a constant undercurrent in earlier Christian history.

In medieval canon law, having had anything to do with shedding blood, even having served on a court to try a person for a capital offense, could disqualify a man for the priesthood. In 988, the first measure taken, to mark his conversion, by Prince Vladimir of Kiev, honored by Russians as their first Christian king, was the elimination of the death penalty.

On January 5, 1527, when Felix Mantz of Zurich was condemned to drowning as the first radical protestant to be executed by a protestant government, part of the accusation was that he testified "that a Christian should not be a ruler, nor execute anyone with the sword, kill or punish . . ." Menno Simons, Frisian leader of a movement like that of Mantz, wrote to the Calvinist Martin Micron in 1556 that civil killing ill becomes a Christian ruler.[6]

When in 1682 William Penn wrote his "Great Act," the Crown charter for his Quaker colony, the death penalty was eliminated for all crimes except premeditated murder, and even that was only included because it was demanded by the Crown. Thus what Beccaria began to articulate in 1764 and Rush in 1787 was but a new phase, adjusted to the age of Enlightenment, of a much older and more specifically Christian tradition of pro-life criticism. That tradition has worn thin recently, as many Christians have not seen past the prevalent linking of faith commitment with political conservatism. Some have oddly thought that concern for the dignity of the life of offenders was incompatible with concern for the wrongness of sin. What our study has shown is that if we take more seriously the original cultural rootedness of the death penalty in primitive rituals of retaliation, we must also acknowledge, in the light of the Cross, our unworthiness to kill even the guilty.

NOTES

1. Cf. J. Yoder, "Exodus 20:13—'Thou shalt not kill.'" in *Interpretation* 34/4 (October 1982), 394ff. Walther Koehler and Brevard Childs are the scholars using this phrase.

2. A collection of quotations in favor of the validity of retribution, as "instinctive" or as socially useful, is presented by Raoul Berger (see bibliography), 135.

3. Therefore I agree with the excellent work of the philosopher Nathanson (see bibliography) that the argument against the death penalty must begin by acknowledging the parcel of truth in the popular demand for it.

4. I have used here the broadest language in order to demonstrate openness to the anthropologist's agenda. The Christian is enabled and commanded to take such sacrificial love as life's law on the grounds of Jesus; yet that does not make it an esoteric notion nor a mystery for others.

5. Concerning the centrality of forgiveness, cf. William Klassen, *The Forgiving Community* (Philadelphia: Westminster, 1966); on the importance of the offender or enemy in locating the meaning of forgiveness, cf. William Klassen, *Love of Enemy; the Way to Peace* (Philadelphia: Fortress, 1984). "Forgive us as we forgive" is the only petition in the Lord's Prayer to be conditional. It is the task for which Jesus empowers his disciples with the gift of the Holy Spirit (John 20:21ff); the activity for which he himself has been most criticized by the authorities (Matt. 9:2ff).

6. Menno gives three reasons: if the offender has repented of his sin you are killing your Christian brother; if he has not, you are consigning him prematurely to hell. Even the pagan Lacedaemonians did not kill offenders, but imprisoned them and put them to work.

RESPONSES

RESPONSE: Unpersuaded

H. WAYNE HOUSE

Entering into this friendly debate with Dr. John Howard Yoder has been a special privilege. Dr. Yoder is known as a theologian of repute; his arguments in this book are standard for the anticapital punishment view and are clear and accurate statements of that view.

The reader should know, however, that even though there is a tradition in the history of the church supporting Dr. Yoder's view, it has never been generally accepted. The majority of the church's theologians, and most Christians, have not found pacifistic arguments very persuasive. Having read carefully Professor Yoder's presentation, I also find the agruments severely lacking in solid biblical support. He has not presented anything new that will convince a person who studies the Scriptures carefully on this subject. In fact, Dr. Yoder's analysis of Scripture may be the weakest portion of his argument. Moreover, attempts to undercut the death penalty position by painting his opponents in extreme positions or with a broad brush, by appealing to questionable sociological data, and by seeking to entice the reader to accept his position by smooth logical moves or generalities belie the weakness of his overall approach.

Before tackling Dr. Yoder's arguments, I will first note points of agreement, or at least of common understanding between Yoder and myself. John Yoder offers a number of key points in his rejection of the death penalty as a viable punishment for any crime today. The most significant area of agreement between us is the identity of our basic position. I argue that in the Noachian Covenant, God established the death penalty as the universally required punishment for willful, deliberate murder, since this covenant was made with all humanity. Yoder acknowledges that this position is "intellectually understandable" (p. 165) but rejects it as a valid interpretation of Genesis 9. At least, however, he understands my basic contention. I have changed my thinking some on this important question. In earlier years I recognized the right of the contemporary state to exercise the death penalty for a variety of reasons. More recently I have become convinced that only crimes that cause death by the design of another person are open to the extreme penalty. Whenever I speak of capital punishment, I am speaking of it as a universally exacted retribution for murder or complicity in murder, nothing more and nothing less.

We also agree that there are major practical problems with the application of capital punishment, whether for murder or any other crime. It is true that our criminal justice system appears at times more criminal than just. However, practical problems do not justify disobedience to divine commands. Thus, while we might expect some practical results from application of biblical teachings, the absence of such in no way vitiates the doctrines involved.

A third area of agreement is his contention (p. 108) that the arguments on capital punishment are more than merely yes or no. To say that one believes in the death penalty does not mean that he or she would agree with every reason for the extreme penalty or with every method used to administer it. On the other hand, if one takes the position against capital punishment the issues are much narrower. If death is not allowed as a penalty then no matter how heinous the crime, or devastating its effects, or how hardened the nature of the criminal, the right of the state to make the punishment fit the crime is forbidden.

Improper Logic

Oftentimes Dr. Yoder makes statements that go against proper logical argument, such as using arguments from silence, omitting a middle position, overgeneralizing, not following implications of a position consistently, or assuming what he seeks to prove. When he speaks of the inadequacy of deterrence on p. 116, he states, "if the deterrent theory were to 'work,' the certainty that every killer will be killed would have to be nearly absolute." This is a straw man argument. He places the argument at the extreme, either all or nothing. This is like saying, "For traffic enforcement to be effective every speeder must be caught." Just the opposite is true. When people see a police car, most slow down. The same is also true of the deterrent value of the death penalty.

Repeatedly on p. 139 Dr. Yoder speaks of what Jesus *could* have said. This is merely speculation on his part, an argument from silence. Yoder seeks to set aside the force of the possible death penalty presented in John 8:1–11, of which I will speak later. But he does not know any more than I what Jesus may or may not have wanted to say. We only have the words recorded by the evangelist John.

In several places he uses circular reasoning about the nature of the death penalty; he assumes what he needs to prove. For example, on p. 155 (see also p. 158) he says about retribution, "Yet, why a second wrong should right the first one is not easily explained." On p. 176 he speaks of the need to put an end to the idea of death as redemption for death (see Num. 35:31), of "putting to an end the mechanisms of mimetic vengeance." In these two examples he wrongly assumes that the death penalty is a wrong and that death for death is not a proper way to deal with murder. He must not merely assume; he must prove it is wrong. Another way he commits this fallacy is in assuming, without proof, that the death penalty by the state is a rejection of Christ's lordship over all of life (p. 144). This is only true if God does not exercise his lordship in the civil realm differently than in the personal realm. A brief example of the difference between these two is illustrated in the life of Christ. Jesus taught that in private relationships when one is insulted (struck on the right cheek) that person is to offer the other cheek. Yet in his trial when he was struck on the cheek he did not turn his cheek but demanded to know the legal basis for the act. These are different spheres for Christ and us, whether in the exercise of rights or the exercise of punishment.

Dr. Yoder develops arguments that, if applied consistently, would contradict the biblical teachings on the substitutionary death of Christ and eternal punishment (p. 149). He speaks of the Cross of Christ often (e.g., 144, 176) but the crucified Christ endured the very penalty which

Yoder rejects. Justice demands payment for sin. God's holy nature had to be satisfied for the awful sins against him. Christ's death does not automatically bring penal forgiveness to murderers any more than his death empties hell. If there is only forgiveness and no justice for crimes committed (p. 176) then God should send everyone to heaven. It is true that Paul says in Romans 1 that all the sins listed are worthy of death—and that under the law of God to Israel many sins would have brought the extreme punishment. But God in the worldwide covenant with Noah, the father of all nations, decreed only death for intentional killing.

Failure to Separate Personal Ethics from State Ethics

Dr. Yoder's first error is his inability to divorce personal ethics from state ethics (p. 109). I do not doubt the sincerity of those who do this nor do I suggest that they are necessarily any less committed to Scripture. Oftentimes, though, they have overemphasized one aspect of the nature of God to the neglect of other attributes. God is not only a God of love. He is also a God of justice. He has commanded each of us as individuals to respond in specific ways to our neighbor. He has not so commanded the state. I do not mean by this that any and everything that the state should decide to do is moral. But I do contend with biblical authority that there is a differentiation between these two ethics. The criminal codes and military policies of Israel were not inventions of that community. They did not decide to use the death penalty in cases of crime or war and then, the nation having done so, the biblical writers put this into the mouth of God. No, God commanded that certain crimes demanded the extreme penalty. There is simply no evidence that God merely allowed for them some kind of inferior ethic in these matters.

The words of Jesus of which Yoder speaks refer not to the functions of the state as a servant of God, but to individual believers in their relationships with others. When he addressed individuals we find that Jesus set forth his teaching on personal ethics from the teaching of the Old Testament. The Jesus who taught love for enemies in the Gospels is the same God who gave that same teaching in the Torah. As well, this same Jesus is the Yahweh of the Old Testament who gave commandments of war and the death penalty to Israel in the Torah. The ethics of God have not changed from the Old Testament to the New; only the specific purposes of God for his people Israel have changed. The ethic of capital punishment and war found in the Old Testament, in reference to state responsibilities, has not been supplanted in the New Testament by a call for personal ethics to be the state's ethics.

The law of God in ancient Israel provided for civil justice to be exercised in numerous instances in ways different from the more general occurrences found among the nations.[1] One crime punishable by death was cursing or striking one's parents (Deut. 21:18–23). In such cases, however, this was not personal vengeance. The parents were required to bring the child (son) before the civil authorities who would try the child and inflict death if he was guilty. It was viewed as good ("so you shall put away the evil *person* from among you," NKJV). The penalty is perceived by God to be a deterrent ("and all Israel shall hear and fear," NKJV) contrary to the many statements to the contrary by Dr. Yoder.

The law of God was plain that one guilty of murder was not to be freed or forgiven. In fact, God warned the children of Israel not to preserve the life of the guilty ("Moreover you shall take no ransom for the life of a murderer who is guilty of death, but he shall be put to death," Num. 35:31 NKJV). God said that to allow a murderer to live would pollute the land (Num. 35:33). Interestingly God's rationale is traced back to his commands to Noah. Observe the parallel:

Gen. 9:5–6: "From the hand of every man's brother I will require the life of man.
Whoever sheds man's blood, by man his blood shall be shed."

Num. 35:33: ". . . for no atonement [satisfaction] can be made for the land[2]
for the blood that is shed on it [the land], except by the blood of him who shed it."

The differentiation of these two ethics so clearly seen in the teaching and practices of the law of Israel is repeated in similar terms in the writings of Paul.

In Romans 12 the apostle speaks of loving enemies, of not taking vengeance since this was only for God to do. Yet in Romans 13 the apostle says that the state is the servant of God to exercise his vengeance. Paul sees no conflict between the two. It is true that there is no certainty, though there is the likelihood, that the sword of Romans 13 refers to the right of the state to use the death penalty. Yoder makes much of the fact, in his perspective, that "sword" in Romans 13 is a dagger (p. 146). This misses the point. The sword, even the short Roman sword, is a symbol for force, even death. Nothing has been gained by his argument. Even if this were not the teaching in Romans 13, no one can deny that God gave this right and duty to Israel. Have God's underlying moral perspectives changed? Hardly. The problem develops when some Christians confuse the personal ethics we are to have and the ethical duty God gave to the state.

Substituting "Humane" Arguments for Biblical Arguments

A third error of Dr. Yoder is his substitution of "general humane arguments" (p. 109) for specific biblical teaching and logical deductions from that teaching. This allows him to "read between the lines" of the various texts and assume what surely could not be true without being held to the clear teaching of the biblical texts.

Seeking to dispel the idea of retribution being a valid punishment, he draws an analogy of spanking children, "A child trained by spanking may grow up to become a teenage gangster or an abusive parent. What beating [he tends to use volatile words] a child teaches most effectively may well be less 'don't get into the cookie jar' than 'might makes right,' or 'if you cannot reason, use force'" (p. 129). The Bible teaches otherwise (Prov. 13:24; 23:13–14).

Dr. Yoder claims that killing a murderer has no deterrence value (pp. 114–16). The Bible makes a contrary claim (Deut. 17:13; 19:20; 21:21).

He views the death penalty as only a cultural reflex (p. 137). The Bible sees it as a valid retribution from a holy God through his agent the state.

He sees capital punishment as an infringement on the holy will of God (p. 140). The Bible views it as the command from this holy God (Gen. 9:6; Num. 35:16–21, 29–34). In these, and other places, Dr. Yoder's opinions do not square with the teachings of God's Word.

188

Relying on Extrabiblical Sources in lieu of Biblical Texts

A fourth error is to give too much credence to extrabiblical sources and arguments in deciding the question of the death penalty. There is no question but that we can benefit from information learned in sociology, criminology, law, and psychology. They may provide understanding into the human mind and human behavior. They may help us determine if proper evidence or procedure have been used in ascertaining the guilt of the one convicted. But they may not be used by the Christian as a substitution for the biblical teaching on this subject. "Let God be true, and every man a liar!" says the apostle (Rom. 3:4 NIV). There can be only one final authority on this matter for the Christian. This is not to say that such an appeal to authority would be accepted in every or any instance by those in government in either proscribing or prohibiting the death penalty. One might use other kinds of argument in the contexts. But in deciding in one's own heart, the Bible is the Christian's authority.

Failure to Properly Harmonize Biblical Teaching

The fifth error of Dr. Yoder is the manner in which he reads and interprets the biblical texts. He believes in an evolution of biblical ethics. Rather than God doing something special in Israel that he has not chosen to do in any other nation, Yoder considers the teaching of Jesus to be a correction to God's laws. Now there is no doubt in my mind that Jesus clarifies the law for the people, and that he corrects the misunderstandings of the law practiced by religious leaders. But his teaching is not new. He, the Yahweh of the Old Testament, gave that law to them before. They failed to practice it. He came to give the Spirit so that our personal ethics through the help of the Spirit would fulfill the law.

Dr. Yoder refuses the universality of the Old Testament's teaching on capital punishment (p. 174). In his statement he fails to reckon with several facts. First, the basis for capital punishment in the Noachian covenant builds not on temporary cultural standards. The basis is mankind's bearing of the image of God. Murder affronts God's image in man and thus God rightly demands justice. The fact that humanity was made in God's image is universal, so the command for capital punishment does not rise from a cultural base.

Second, the Noachian covenant came to Noah as the head of the new human race. Abraham, the father of Israel, had not yet been called. God did not issue a temporary national guideline (albeit Israel did have detailed and unique applications of that underlying moral law) to one nation among many, but rather he declared a command to the new beginning of all races.

Third, Yoder implies that capital punishment is a cultural norm much like slavery and polygamy in ancient times (p. 159). Nowhere does God command such cultural failings, but he did require capital punishment. Yoder does not differentiate between divine imperatives and cultural shortcomings in the Old Testament.

Fourth, he ignores the boundless principle underlying the Mosaic Law commands. True, the law was fulfilled in Christ and no one is bound to its specific civil legislation, but the universal principle of the Noachian Covenant was not invalidated at the Cross.

God created man in his own image. He requires retribution when that image is effaced in murder. This universal theological precept forms the foundation for capital punishment for society as a whole. The precept finds expansion in the Mosaic Law, which law was fulfilled in Christ. However, the principle itself remains as substantiated by the acknowledged legitimacy of capital punishment in Romans 13:1–4. If retribution as a principle died at the Cross, then Paul would have never supported the right of a civil authority to punish crime. In fact, if punishment for crime was annulled in Jesus' death, then no civil authority has the right to penalize any offender for any crime. Paul clearly saw the spiritual forgiveness of sin through the Cross *and* the necessary retribution for crime by civil authorities.

Failure to Separate Administration of
Justice from the Need for Justice

Yoder raises the substantive issue of the practical effects of the death penalty. Some statistics regarding capital punishment seem to indicate that it is ineffective in deterring crime and that those political groups— be they states or societies—which do not enforce the death penalty have less crime than those which do. I acknowledge that capital punishment has often been improperly applied according to the terms of the Noachian Covenant. Consequently the available statistics demonstrate the results of this *improper* application and offer no basis for evaluating the results of a *proper* enforcement of the death penalty.

Yoder further argues that capital punishment should not, cannot, and does not deter crime. Consequently, he maintains, the death penalty should be rejected. Again, we point to the fact that little evidence exists concerning the results of the proper application of capital punishment. I believe that the proper enforcement of the death penalty *would* serve as an effective deterrent to crime. The deterrent value of capital punishment, however, is a subsidiary benefit and not a justification for its enforcement.

Let me first speak to the question of impractical or improper application of biblical commands. Just because policemen do not equitably distribute traffic tickets does not mean that traffic laws or penalties are bad. A parallel situation exists with capital punishment. Even though there is no absolute certainty in the justice system, there are more than sufficient safeguards to protect the person who might be charged with such crimes against the likelihood of receiving the ultimate judgment. The perfect state does not exist, but the responsibility of the state to mete out the justice of God (Rom. 13:1–5) remains. The basic issue is whether or not God requires the death penalty for murderers today. If the Bible clearly shows that he does, then the issue is settled. If, on the other hand, the Bible shows he has commanded that capital punishment not be applied today, then, again, the issue is settled. Only if the Bible is silent on the subject do other arguments take on significant importance. It is my contention that God is not silent on the matter and that he does require capital punishment today for murder. Any lack of practical benefits is the result of problems in administration and application of the death penalty.

I have referred several times to the concept of the "correct application" of the death penalty without stating what I mean by these terms. Capital punishment, indeed any punishment, must be applied for the correct reason. Yoder seems to indicate that the basic motivation for punishment of any kind is to deter further wrongdoing. I argue that the foundational motive for punishment is retribution, not deterrence. To restate the points made in my section of this book, retribution means that an individual earns punishment for a deliberate act against agreed-upon rules of conduct. Retribution is *not* vengeance on either the personal or the societal levels; it is not appeasement of angry deities; nor is it a ritual designed to right some cosmic balance that was tipped by the crime. Retribution is the payment of something earned by a specific act. As I have already shown, it is the consistent biblical theory of punishment and the foundational principle for capital punishment.

Questionable Understanding of Biblical Texts

Dr. Yoder has taken positions on certain biblical texts which simply are difficult to sustain exegetically. Certainly others have shared his interpretations but they are special pleadings of the texts that reflect a bias requiring a misreading of the words and contexts of the passages.

Since space does not allow interaction with every scripture on which I disagree with Yoder's interpretations, I will address only his handling of Genesis 9, John 8, and Romans 13. He identifies Genesis 9:1–6, the Noachian Covenant, as descriptive, not determinative; as ritualistic, not governmental. He argues that this passage continues the sacrifice theme introduced in 8:20 by describing the killing of animals for food in terms of ritual sacrifices. There is no "secular slaughtering," Yoder claims (p. 123), for all killing is seen in terms of sacrifice. This concept extends to the killing of humans. Whenever a killing is avenged by another death, a sacrifice has been made. Genesis 9:6, a record of "oral lore, cited by sages and priests" (p. 120), merely describes what is already occurring and reemphasizes the sacrificial nature of such an act.

Genesis 9:1–6 and its wider context does not support this interpretation. In 8:20 Noah builds an altar and offers sacrifices to Yahweh. The Lord accepts the sacrifices and makes a specific promise: no more universal floods. The poetic structure of verse 22 may reflect the popular expression of this promise in Moses' day, but this structure does not mean that the truths expressed are not revelation to Noah and his family. They had just come through the Deluge and may well have wondered about Yahweh's attitude toward them. This promise assures them that this destructive event was unique. Creation will continue in its regular course of seasons as long as the earth exists. Noah and his family need not fear another destructive flood.

Chapter 9 continues the narrative by relating events subsequent to the sacrifices of Genesis 8:20. Yahweh established new relationships between Noah and the animate creation. Animals will now fear mankind, and justly so, for mankind is authorized to kill them for food. "But you must not eat meat that has its lifeblood still in it" (9:4 NIV). Does this prohibition mean that the blood is sacred, something that is to be poured out in sacrifice to Yahweh at every killing for food? Or does it mean that animal life is to be respected as it is used? Yoder argues that the sacrificial setting of chapter 8 supports the former. We argue that the extension of the concept of sacrifice from chapter 8 into chapter 9 is not justified by the text. The introduction of new material indicates another part of the narrative, one that transpires after the sacrifices. Yahweh permits the killing of animals for food, but he is not claiming their poured-out blood as a sacrifice. He does not demand an accounting for every animal killed.

What, then, about the killing of humans in light of this new prohibition? Certainly Genesis 4:23–24 shows that blood vengeance was already practiced, in spite of the mercy shown to Cain (Gen. 4:15). Does Yahweh's permission to kill animals extend to humans? No, clearly it does not, for the unique nature of mankind as the divine image-bearer distinguishes him from the animals. God affirms this distinction by demanding an accounting of all human blood shed, whether by human or animal agency. Yahweh is establishing a new relationship and a new responsibility. He is not merely describing the usual course of events. In point of fact, there are no usual events to describe, for Noah and his family are alone, for the former society had been destroyed by the Deluge. Now, at the start of a new era, God invests the human race with new privileges and new accountability.

Are we to understand this shedding of the murderer's blood as personal vengeance or as retribution enacted by formalized systems of justice? The narrative gives no direct information one way or another, but Yahweh's later development of capital punishment in the Mosaic Code shows that the death penalty is to be applied by government, not individuals. Certainly, as Yoder notes, the division between priest and president, between ceremonial and civil, was not as wide in the theocracy as in modern governmental systems. But when legal cases were brought to the priests in the theocracy they relied on the written

Scriptures, case law, or direct revelation to guide their decisions. Consequently we argue that Genesis 9 establishes the basis for the governmental application of the death penalty in the case of first-degree murder.

We must emphasize that the death penalty is the prerogative of government, not individuals. Clearly governments are established by God to do what individuals cannot or should not do by themselves. A proper government, among other things, collects taxes and punishes wrongdoers, as Paul writes in Romans 13:1–7. One of the proper exercises of divinely established governmental authority, we argue, is the application of capital punishment for murder. Capital punishment is not the legalized killing of individuals by individuals. It is the payment of the divinely established penalty, death, for the willful murder of another human being by divinely established governments. Certainly people, such as soldiers, police, and tax collectors, carry out the decrees of government. Such people, in the exercise of their governmental authority, can do things that would be illegal for them to do as private individuals.

This is exactly what Paul is stating in Romans. Paul forbids individuals from exercising wrath in personal revenge and admonishes them to let God avenge evil deeds (Rom. 12:19). One of God's agents of wrath by which he avenges evil deeds is human government, for its officials are "agents of wrath" to punish evildoers (Rom. 13:4). Such officials may even exercise the authority of the sword, i.e., of capital punishment. Yoder denies that the term "sword" (*machaira*) refers to execution, noting that this "is the symbol of judicial authority, not the weapon of either war or the death penalty" (p. 146). Paul, however, uses *machaira* in his list of armament in Ephesians 6:17 and Luke describes the execution of James with the same term (Acts 12:2). *Machaira* in Romans 13:4 can be seen as a reference to the government's proper authority to execute criminals. Capital punishment is a proper exercise of governmental authority, not individual vengeance, and is carried out, at least in the case of murder, in obedience to God's command.

While we agree with John Yoder that the Mosaic Code has no direct application beyond Old Testament Israel, we disagree with his claim that Jesus overturned capital punishment in either his teaching or his cross-work. Clearly the book of Hebrews shows that the sacrifice of Jesus completed the sacrificial system by cleansing, not just covering sin. Yoder claims that this also ended capital punishment, but he bases this claim on the identification of killing as a sacrificial act. We have shown that Genesis 9 makes no such claim for killing, either of animals or mankind. Neither the killing of animals for food or executing murders in retribution are ritual, sacrificial acts. Consequently, the sacrifice of Jesus on the Cross does not cancel the moral law demanding capital punishment before the law was given to Israel. The very moral principle that calls for the Cross—the principle of life for life—is the same principle behind capital punishment. If Yoder's view were correct, the substitutionary atonement of Christ would be incorrect.

Yoder also claims that Jesus set aside capital punishment when he encountered the adulterous woman and her accusers, as described in John 8:1–11. Yoder correctly identifies the problem as a challenge to Jesus' authority, not as an innocent question of the Mosaic Code. The authority Jesus claimed, however, was not governmental or social, as Yoder claims (p. 139). Jesus, as recognized by some in his audience (John 4:26; 7:41), claimed to be the Christ, the Messiah. This was a clear claim to spiritual, not governmental authority. He is the King of kings, but his exercise of authority over the kingdoms of men will come in the future establishment of his kingdom.

Jesus' response to the woman's accusers is the oft-quoted "If any one of you is without sin, let him be the first to throw a stone at her" (John 8:7 NIV). He is not, contrary to Yoder's assertion, "challenging the self-ascribed righteousness of those who claim the authority to kill others" (p. 140). First of all, no one acting as an individual has any authority to kill anyone else, except, perhaps, in self-defence, which is beyond our discussion. Authority to carry out the death penalty comes from government in the exercise of its divinely ordained mandate to apply capital punishment to murderers. Jesus is not challenging nor changing any governmental authority, nor are the Pharisees tempting him to do so. They are trying to force him to contradict either the law of Moses or of Rome. He refused to contradict either. Instead, he confronted the self-ascribed righteousness of these religious leaders who sought to twist the Mosaic Code to their own advantage. Jesus did not have to cite the requirement to stone both adulterous partners—the lawyers and the Pharisees all knew the law, probably from memory. Jesus claimed religious authority and on that basis he confronted this pompous display of hypocrisy. The accusers recognized his point and left. Jesus' words to the woman, "Go now and leave your life of sin," (John 8:11 NIV) are no more a rejection of government's authority to inflict capital punishment than they are approval of adultery. His forgiveness of her sin in no way vitiates the prescribed penalty in particular nor governmental authority in general.

Another point to consider in Yoder's argument is his assertion, "If the death penalty is understood as an act of God (as it certainly was in ancient Israel), then the judge and executioner must be morally above reproach." This is true in the sense of being honest about evaluating the evidence fairly and giving true testimony at trial. Never does the law of God require absolute or general moral purity to judge another or to put to death a convicted person deserving of death. If it did, no justice would ever be executed since we are all morally imperfect beings.

We have argued that God established capital punishment as the retribution for murder as part of the Noachian Covenant and that that authority continues to this day as part of governmental responsibility. We have maintained that Jesus did not change this authority, either in his teaching or in his sacrifice. We have further argued that Paul confirmed the continuation of this authority on the part of government.

John Yoder, obviously, has argued for a different position. It is our fervent hope and prayer that everyone who claims Christ as Lord and Savior will not accept one position or the other because of human authority, but that they will turn to his Word for themselves and let their own study, perhaps catalyzed by this discussion, persuade them. Ultimately each of us will give an account for our own beliefs and actions. If this discussion has motivated you in the right direction, then to God be the glory!

NOTES

1. I discuss the reasons for this in my book *Dominion Theology: Blessing or Curse?* (Portland, Ore.: Multnomah Press, 1988).

2. Compare Genesis 5:10–11 where God personally makes an exception before the command to Noah in Genesis 9:6. Even here, though, the natural law within man assumed the death penalty.

RESPONSE: Closer Than It Seemed

JOHN HOWARD YODER

Dr. House has presented a careful and, at points, original argument. First, let me note, without attention to detail, the points on which Dr. House and I agree.

- We reject the "theonomic" notion that all the laws of Moses should be applied by all human governments[1].
- Deterrence, one of the two major arguments given in favor of the death penalty, is immoral in itself (although House still argues at length that it is a desirable side effect which results from applying capital punishment on other grounds).[2]
- Efforts to determine on social-science grounds whether the existence of death penalty legislation deters premeditated killing have not proven anything firm.[3]

One of the drawbacks of this model of interlocking authorship is that both Dr. House and I had to provide some of the same historical and legal background. The reader will note some differences between the two accounts, but they are of limited significance for the debate. I shall not use space in this response to discuss them further.[4]

Nor do I like to take much space for "debating" responses in the style imposed on me by the debate format. Yet, at some points I must label specific weaknesses of the way he makes his case.[5]

House's text abounds in references to the arguments of others: "some say" and "many say. . . ." These are mostly opinions which are not cited, and often his playback does not seem to me to represent the literature. Surely he is trying to be fair. But he states them in the way that best sets up his response. Some of the arguments he seeks to refute are not my own (so I don't defend them here against his criticism). Yet I should warn readers that the adequacy of those summaries would be contested by others.

At just one point I must object more directly to his "straw man" style. At least three times (pp. 3, 47, 74) he suggests that opposition to the death penalty is based on a naive literalism about the Sixth Commandment. "Who can debate such clear commands?" Then he knocks it down by saying that God himself would be a transgressor, because of the wars and the capital punishment texts in the same biblical passage, as if anyone were unaware of that contradiction. I know of no prolife argument which is thus naive either in fact or in intention.[6]

Disentangling "Retribution" from Everything Else

I am sure that Dr. House is sincere and honest in the central verbal move he makes, but logically it is still a trick. Historically it ignores the record, and bypasses the issues raised by the understanding of the death penalty which dominates our culture.

"Retaliation" is in ordinary language the normal word for any punishment which fits the crime. "Retribution" or "punishment" is that subset of retaliation where the "payment" has legal backing. When it is possible to restore to the victim what had been wrongly taken it can be called "restitution" or "restoration." "Vengeance" is the cultural anthropological description of why individuals and societies desire retaliation and legalize retribution. Within a religious worldview it tends to coincide with "expiation." The several terms designate different dimensions of what societies experience as one reality.

House pulls this entire coherent social system apart by a purely arbitrary, purely mental act of definition.[7] He rejects the word *retaliation* without any clear argument, yet he keeps its Latin equivalent *lex talionis* (p. 22). He continues to use, in favor of what he calls "retribution," the arguments which for others support "retaliation." He sweepingly rejects "vengeance" as an unworthy moral justification for the death penalty, yet he grants that vengeance is the main reason for which societies do, in fact, kill people (and a major explanation of how they decide which people to kill when most killers are not executed). Thus the death penalty which he advocates is not the one which is in effect in the U.S.A.

This definitional gambit is doubly misleading. (a) It gives the unsuspecting reader the idea that the separation of concepts which he proposes was always there, is socially warranted, and clarifies issues. (b) It moves the discussion, without avowing it, away from the real world of American legal practices. House makes a theoretical case for *both* a concept and a practice which do not exist. To this latter question I shall need to return.

History and Hermeneutics

A simple way to characterize House's approach is that he reads the Bible backwards, from the present to Genesis. He begins with a modern vision of individual human dignity, according to which a central dimension of the person is the duty to pay for one's misdeeds. Thus, to punish a person, to harm a person, even to the point of death, is, House claims, a service to that person's dignity thus defined, and is therefore a positive moral act. The best statement of this point of view is a few lines from C. S. Lewis, which House cites at least seven times, not quite fairly.[8]

Only after having set up the argument in terms of a modern notion of individual dignity does House turn to the Bible to support what he has already decided. He walks back through the centuries and the covenants, finding it possible to fit this modern notion to what he finds there, sometimes ignoring and sometimes denying the differences which historians care about. Without really noticing it, he leaps over the cultural anthropologists' understanding of retribution as protecting the dignity not of the sinner but of the social order and its present rulers.

He does not leap over those strands of Scripture and culture where it is the gods or God who demands retribution; but as his argument proceeds, it oscillates between the dignity of God who demands punishment and that of the guilty human who needs it. These are not the same. One is modern, the other ancient. Sometimes those two arguments coincide, of course, but they differ when the God in question is a God who exercises mercy.[9] They differ as well when the guilty human is destroyed.

This approach "back from the present" results in House's claim to find in Genesis 9 a charter for civil order in all times and places.[10] This is something no reader without a preformed grid would find there. Because the grid came from the twentieth century, there can be no development. There can be other covenants, other laws, House grants, but this one is immutable.

At this point Dr. House speaks for a very special, very modern subculture, narrower than fundamentalism in general, narrower than dispensationalism in general, though not as narrow as the "theonomic" alternative to which he devotes some space. I honor his freedom to belong to the intellectual world which he has chosen, and to believe as he does, but the reader needs to be warned that thereby some of the pro-death arguments in the mainstream debate, which make more of the Mosaic material than he does, are not represented.[11]

My approach, on the other hand, was the more ordinary one of coming through history, including the Bible as history, beginning at the beginning. I found that the phenomenon of retaliation was present in Genesis well before Noah, as it is present in all ancient and primitive cultures. René Girard has joined the anthropological guild in telling us how the death penalty worked as a safeguard for simple societies. Genesis 4 (which House does not read closely) shows both God's first act of saving a murderer from death and a heroic case of seven-fold retaliation. Development is not only permissible but natural, even imperative, not only from Cain to Noah to Abraham to Moses to Jeremiah to Jesus, as the record shows, but also since the apostles stopped writing.

The Christian message has covered the earth, transforming as it went the cultures it found. Sometimes believers sold out to the pagan patterns their message met—that is why there needs often to be a return to biblical basics. Other times the progress is authentic, a prolongation of a biblical line. Specimens of such progress in the light of human dignity under God were the concept of government as a covenant with the governed, religious liberty and equality before the law, and the creation of bills of rights and constitutions. Each such new value is human, each has its shadow side, but when we welcome such a step, the fact that it was not commanded in Genesis or in Acts does not count against it. Another specimen is the wave of revulsion which swept most death penalty laws from the books in Britain in the nineteenth century[12], as well as the slower, broader wave which has completely removed the death penalty in most democracies.

House simply disregards the issue of how to evaluate historical change from a biblical perspective, although at numerous points he makes without argument assumptions drawn from the modern Western justice tradition. He can ignore it because his vision of moral legislation is timeless. House believes he should ignore historical change (one odd exception being the impact of the Norman feudal patterns on English legal concepts),[13] since he believes the Bible is timeless. Thus it is natural for him, even when he goes to the trouble to review the social science data on deterrence or the debate about the U.S. Constitution, to conclude that those arguments do not really matter, and to shrug off as immaterial the many discrepancies between our society's practice of the death penalty and what he claims would theoretically be morally valid.

The very shape of the Bible, written as a story and not a code, makes me confess that if God has led people in a particular direction through a story, he was not going to become another kind of God two or three generations after Pentecost when the last apostle wrote his last word. God is faithful to himself, but that fidelity is an integrity of ongoing purpose, not a timeless immutability. Later changes were not all for the good, as a naive doctrine of progress might say (but not really believe). Nor were they all for the worse. Nor do I believe that it belongs to the bishop of Rome to decide which changes were right.

The only solution to the challenge of change, between timelessness and accepting whatever happens as "progress," is the open-ended one of testing all things for whether they are compatible with Christ (1 Cor. 12:1-3, 1 John 4:1-2), holding to whatever stands the tests (Phil. 4:8) of being true, honorable, just, pure, lovely, gracious, excellent, or praiseworthy. House rejects this kind of historical consciousness —even concerning the U.S. Constitution—as if it were unbelief. By the nature of the case there is thus no basis for extending beyond our two original texts the argument about this contrast of mental styles.

THE DEATH PENALTY DEBATE

The "Real World" Test

House's unconcern for discrepancies is especially disconcerting when he comes to the data about innocent victims. He undervalues the numbers and dodges most of the literature, but at least he does not deny that some innocent persons are killed by the state due to judicial errors and/or false accusations. Then he shrugs it off by saying that there are many other less-than-capital miscarriages of justice which cannot be made right either. What does that have to do with the wrongness of murder at the hand of the state, i.e., in our name? It is House, not the abolitionists, who make the claim for the absolute divine imperative of restitution. Who then pays the retribution for the people murdered in our name? It is House who claims the dignity of human life as the unique protected value, the protection of which is qualitatively different from all the other values protected by the threat of death in the Mosaic legislation, which he does not advocate applying. This is contradicted by his flippant claim that the state's killing of the innocent does not matter because other injustices are irreparable too.

Whenever the issue arises, House excuses from the duty of retribution those whose act of homicide was not intended. His argument applies only to premeditated killing. This fits with the modern humanist view of retribution as due to the offender's dignity, and with some modern law, but not with the absolute divine imperative House claims to see in Genesis 9. What House does not do at all is provide any help with problems of diminished capacity. He expressly limits his arguments to coolly premeditated murder, without even being clear on whether his argument for the death penalty applies to crimes committed in a burst of passion (p. 88). If an "imbecile" or a child is excusable, at what level of age or IQ does the absolute of Genesis 9 begin? Crimes of passion are often mitigated by the claim of "temporary insanity," opening a large can of psychological and jurisprudential worms. House avoids this field, since his concepts do not help to deal with it; but the reader and the citizen must face it. House is also quite free in acknowledging that guilty individuals may properly be freed from punishment (Cain, David, the woman in John 8), but refuses to see that when the merciful authority doing that is God, the event is pertinent to the question of what God's law demands.

Responses

Final Consensus

Despite the weighty differences between us in intellectual method and in understandings of biblical fidelity, I welcome Dr. House's agreeing with me (as do many of the people he quotes):

- that vengeance in fact motivates many of our fellow citizens who support the death penalty;
- that this reason is morally unworthy;
- that the move from the victim-based concept to king-based concepts of the claim for justice comes not from God but from the Romans and the Normans;[14]
- that retribution *as he defines it and justifies it* is not the present American legal practice;
- that the present American practice of criminal justice is discriminatory in terms of race and class;[15]
- that conservative rules of evidence for the protection of the accused, such as those which he says released the woman in John 8, may enable numerous guilty killers to escape execution; a considerable mitigation of the divine demand for retribution.

House passes off, almost flippantly, as if it were someone else's problem, the discrepancies between the theoretical norm he elaborates and the real world, what he calls the distance between concept and application (76). He ignores the general lay sense of fairness according to which a long and wide experience of unfair application invalidates even the most theoretically acceptable rules. He accepts the existence of the death penalty in our laws, in the states where it exists, even though neither the reason for it nor the way it is applied in our world fits his theory. He shows no interest in either a more "just" or a more "compassionate" clarification of the considerations of diminished capacity, temporary insanity, non-premeditation, and plea bargaining, which, in fact, mean that even in death penalty states only a few killers are in fact killed. He does not argue for removal of laws which provide the death penalty for offenses other than premeditated murder.[16] He does not call Christian citizens to organize missions and lobbies to restore the death penalty in the states (and in all the other modern democracies) where it is not on the books, and to multiply twentyfold the execution rate where it is legal. He does not create action agencies and raise funds to provide more staff for prosecutors in contested cases, counterbalancing the way the campaign against the death penalty was carried on in the courts by legal aid agencies, especially before 1972. He avoids completely the enormous problems waiting in the wings as our society moves toward recriminalizing abortion *as murder*.

My point is not that Dr. House should have done all of this in some specific way. On the contrary; the fact that he was not driven, by the momentum of his own argument, to do most of it, is further proof that what he supports is not an immediate program for America, and certainly not aid and comfort to the pro-death penalty agitators.

The case he makes is an abstract theoretical one. In a culture nonexistent today—in which penalties would be applied dispassionately, promptly, without vengeful glee, without respect of persons, and only to persons fairly proven guilty of premeditation, by judges having nonviolently convinced their unbelieving fellow-citizens that the single story of Genesis 9 should count as charter for all the governments of the world—*then* and only then his case would be coherent.

It is clear that for Dr. House that kind of timeless and placeless coherence, independent of the need for real-world validation or for seeming to be fair to underdogs, is valuable. For me it is not only not valuable, not only not convincing; it constitutes a further piece in the argument on my side. In the real United States of America, violence-ridden and vengeance-ridden as it is, to say as House does that *the only morally valid basis* for the death penalty is the dispassionate defense of the dignity of the offender, counts more against than for the system we now have.

The culture, which by House's own account has never existed, that would practice this kind of enlightened personalism would be better than the one we have in many ways. If I were not a disciple of Jesus, convinced that the Cross both presupposes the notion of retribution (as House agrees) and terminates it (a gospel theme which House notices[17] but does not discuss), I might be willing to test the trust that van den Haag and C. S. Lewis put in rigorous retribution.

NOTES

1. This statement about the Mosaic material is very clear at crucial points; yet elsewhere in the argument he frequently uses Mosaic texts as if he had not set them aside. House says on page 10 that in the entire Mosaic legislation there are twenty-one capital offenses; on pages 101–102 he says "almost twenty". There are more; see page 207.

2. I am not sure that all of the argument of pages 84ff. about deterrence is compatible with what House had said before. The promises that once a punishment has been applied there will be no more sin (Deut. 17:13, 19:20) can hardly be taken literally.

3. It is odd that after devoting four pages to the social-science evidence which is inconclusive, he thinks that with fifteen lines citing the common-sense views of one sheriff and one prosecutor (which he calls "anecdotal evidence") his "point has been made" (p. 88).

4. Nor shall I review the two-pronged legal argument that (a) the U.S. Constitution must not be appealed to in favor of anything that the original drafters did not think about, and (b) that when so read, the Constitution does not consider the death penalty "cruel and unusual." Dr. House has every right to hold such minority legal views, but more argument would be needed for them to have standing in the present discussion. Cf. note 15 below, concerning his lesser regard for the original intent of the Fourteenth Amendment.

5. I cannot take space to argue in detail the number of biblical references which seem to me to be unfair to the text. I must, however, call attention to the fact that in the passages which are not directly exegetical Dr. House uses a prooftexting style which does not always attend to authorial context and intent. Examples are:

- "Under the law of Christ," 1 Cor. 9:21 (p. 4), does not mean an angle on criminal law, nor does it mean "what God has said about the death penalty."
- The Mosaic provision for paying back stolen animals (Exod. 22:1, p. 21) is restoration, not retribution. Restoration or restitution belongs in a general theory of corrections (House omits it in his list of reasons for punishment, 8ff. and again on 16ff), but it cannot be done for murder.
- Romans 7:1 and Colossians 2:16 are not about the *judicial* authority of the law (60).
- The point of Luke 12:47–48 (p. 21) is not that punishment is retributive but that its severity depends on the offender's awareness.
- There is no textual basis for inserting the distinction between premeditated and unpremeditated into Genesis 9:6 (p. 56, note 2). The same insertion is made (p. 49) with the silly statement "it is unreasonable to suppose that God is forbidding accidents." What is at issue is not what God forbids but what should be punished, and House knows that non-premeditation does not always exonerate.

- What Paul says about "law" in Galatians 3 and Romans 6 (p. 10) is not concerned with the theme of punitive civil law.
- The three "eye for eye" passages (p. 27f.) are, as I demonstrated at length (above, p. 133ff.), by no means either in content or in style "a summation of Israel's revealed legal system."
- Jesus did not "physically beat those with whom he disagreed" (quoted with apparent agreement from Bailey, p. 61) when he used a cord to move the animals he had freed.
- Neither in Deuteronomy 22 (cited from Davis) nor in Deuteronomy 19 (cited by House, p. 64) is the death penalty prescribed for failing to bring to court both parties to an act of adultery.

6. There are those who, with theological integrity, argue that the Decalog is on another level, as revelatory of the nature and purposes of God, than the rest of the rules of the Pentateuch. There are those who resolve the tension among the diverse modes of God's acting in more nuanced ways than does House. His straw argument does not recognize nor answer them.

7. The sources he uses, pages 27ff., do not support this split.

8. Lewis expressly disavowed the intent to participate in the debate on capital punishment then going on in Great Britain. His argument was against what he called the "humanitarian theory" used in favor of replacing punishment (i.e., incarceration for a defined time) by indefinite sentencing (*of the living*) in the name of "therapy" or "rehabilitation"; that does not speak to the question of the morality of killing. An argument appealing to the dignity of the person in favor of punishment, as a treatment more befitting the dignity of the guilty person than therapy, cannot function logically to justify destroying the person, and Lewis did not so use it. Nor did he discuss why incarceration is the right retribution in the first place. In his whole prolific career, Lewis published a dozen pages on this topic.

9. House is correct in saying (p. 23) that "justice" and "mercy" are one within the divine nature. That is not the present point. My reference here is to specific accounts of God's dealing with a guilty individual nonretributively.

10. I must guess why he does not go back to Genesis 4, which deals with premeditated murder and the death penalty, or to Genesis 1, where the "image of God" is defined in the first place, or to Genesis 3:16f. which defines fallen history. Against the Reformed tradition, House claims (p. 37) that Genesis 9 is God's first recorded covenant with mankind.

11. My text did something similar by concentrating on what I see as the theological crux of the problem, not reproducing some of the arguments which are current in the wider liberal culture. I do not consider those other arguments wrong. In the frame of reference of secular democracy, they are valid. Yet to evaluate them fairly would call for a more nuanced conversational style than the present frame of reference would permit.

12. Cf. Arthur Koestler in the bibliography.

13. I use the term "odd" here in the technical sense it has in careful dialog; it identifies a position which does not cohere with the bulk of the argument.

Responses

In the face of his many other statements about appealing only to biblical authority, it is hard to understand how House explains the validity of the shift, in the early Middle Ages in Britain, utterly without biblical warrant, from corrections in the interest of the victim to punishment in the name of the state.

14. I am not enough of a lawyer to test this part of his account in detail. I take his word for it, and take it more seriously than he seems to as a criticism of present practice.

15. Although he argues at length the most conservative "original intent" understanding of "cruel and unusual" in the First Amendment, he avoids attending to the meaning of "equal protection under the law" in the Fourteenth.

16. House indicated (p. 8) that he would return to the question of other capital crimes, as well as to the mode of execution, but he does not.

17. The brief "notice" is on page 41. It is set aside by means of a single citation from Baker of a circular argument which contrasts expiation to punishment. This distinction is not in the biblical text (note the importance of the sacrificial language in Genesis 9 about the blood belonging to God) and it contradicts House's use of Hebrews 2 and Romans 3 (p. 29). The reason House does not discuss the witness of Hebrews, although he is aware of it, is that his prior decision, to the effect that there must be a timeless *civil* charter, does not permit him to affirm, as do the apostles, that the Cross and resurrection of Jesus change not only the heart and the guilt status of the believer, but also the cosmos. When he uses the in-group phrase "cross-work of Jesus" (p. 59) he means something much smaller than did the apostles.

The Scope of the Death Penalty
in the Books of Moses

1. Anyone but the priests touching tabernacle furniture (Num. 1:51, 3:10, 38, 4:15, 18:7)
2. Priests drunk on duty (Lev. 10:8–11)
3. Blaspheming the holy Name (Lev. 24:16)
4. Sabbath breaking (Exod. 31:14, 35:2)
5. False prophecy (Deut. 13:1ff, 18:20)
6. Idolatry (Exod. 20:1ff, 22:20; Deut. 13:1–19, 17:2–7)
7. Sorcery (Exod. 22:18; Lev. 20:6, 27)
8. Cursing one's father or mother (Exod. 21:17; Lev. 20:9)
9. Striking one's father or mother (Exod. 21:15)
10. An incorrigible son (Deut. 21:18ff)
11. Murder (Exod. 21:12; Lev. 24:17; Num. 35:16ff)
12. Kidnapping (Exod. 21:16; Deut.24:7)
13. False witness in a capital case (Deut. 19:16–21)

14. Adultery (Lev. 20:10; Deut. 22:22ff)

15. Incest (Lev. 20:11, 17f, 19ff). There is no word for "incest"—the rules simply list ten different forbidden relationships.

16. Sex of man with man (Lev. 20:13)

17. Sex during menstruation (Lev. 20:18)

18. Sex with an animal (Exod. 22:19; Lev. 20:15f.)

19. Prostitution by a priest's daughter (Lev. 21:9; Deut. 22:13–21)

20. Rape (Deut 22:25)

21. Contemptuous disobedience to a court (Deut. 17:8–13)

22. Keeping a dangerous ox (Exod. 21:29)

23. Negligence leading to loss of life (Exod. 21:28f; Deut. 22:8)

24. Failing to bring to trial both parties caught in the act of adultery. House (p. 64) claims this was a capital offense, but the texts he cites do not support it.

25. Sacrificing one's child to Molech (Lev. 20:1f)

26. A wife falsely claiming to be a virgin (Deut. 22:13–21)

There are other commands to kill which are too contextual to be called "legislation": e.g., anyone touching Mount Sinai (Exod. 19:12f). There are also acts of killing guilty persons which were divinely commanded, or are recounted with the narrator's approbation.

House (p. 10) designates items 1, 3, and 4 above as "cultural." There is no indication of what that means. The ancient texts recognize no separations among cult, culture, the moral, and the civil.

Select Annotated Bibliography

This listing is intended to guide readers interested in further study. It therefore includes texts not dealt with in this book. Descriptive notes are added to guide the further research of interested readers. Not all works cited in the text of our arguments are included. Except for a few classics, the listing is limited to the United States, even though related experiences in Canada, the British Isles, and Western Europe ought to be relevant to our discussion. There has been no effort to cover popular periodicals or law journals. Many of the following books include their own bibliographies.

Abel, Charles F., and Frank H. Marsh. *Punishment and Restitution: A Restitutionary Approach to Crime and the Criminal*. Westport, Conn.: Greenwood Press, 1984.

Amnesty International. *United States of America: the Death Penalty*. London, 1987. A survey of the contemporary legal status of death penalty law, including (pp. 162–77), "General Arguments for and against the death penalty."

Bailey, Lloyd R. *Capital Punishment: What the Bible Says*. Nashville: Abingdon Press, 1987. Survey of the relevant biblical passages, with special argument against frequent illegitimate proof-texting, especially when used to ignore the obvious presence of the death penalty in the New Testament.

Baker, William H. *Worthy of Death*. Chicago: Moody Press, 1973.

Barth, Karl. "The Command of God the Creator." In *Church Dogmatics*. Vol. 3/4. Edinburgh: Clark, 1961. The most ambitious and inclusive Protestant theological system of our century, dealing with "Freedom for Life," pp. 324–564, and "Protection of Life," 397–469. The death penalty is treated on pp. 437ff.

Beccaria, Cesare. *On Crimes and Punishments* (1764), new translation. Indianapolis: Bobbs-Merrill, 1963. Europe's first general program for enlightened reforms of the entire penal system, honored by numerous rulers of the epoch. Only pp. 45–52 make the case against the death penalty. "It seems to me absurd that the laws . . . which detest and punish homicide, should themselves commit it, and that to deter citizens from murder, they order a public one (p. 50)."

Bedau, Hugo A. *Death Is Different: Studies in the Morality, Law, and Politics of Capital Punishment*. Boston: Northeastern University Press, 1987. A collection of occasional essays by Bedau himself, on special aspects of the movement. More often Bedau has contributed as an anthology editor (see below).

Bedau, Hugo A., and Chester M. Pierce, eds. *Capital Punishment in the United States*. New York: AMS Press, 1975. Twenty-five social studies on the practice and impact of capital punishment. Quite distinct from the other collection edited by Bedau (see below), it does not include advocacy, moral or religious evaluation, or investigative reporting.

Bedau, Hugo A., and Michael L. Radelet. "Miscarriages of Justice in Potentially Capital Cases." *Stanford Law Review* 40, no. 1 (November 1987): 21–180. The authors attempt to move the study of such cases from the anecdotal level of the studies of Borchard and Frank (see below) to the level of detail which would permit statistical analysis. They found 350 cases in the U.S. courts since 1900 where the fact of miscarriage of justice was documented after initial condemnation. Of these, 116 were in fact condemned to death and 23 were wrongfully executed.

Bedau, Hugo A., ed. *The Death Penalty in America*. 3d ed. New York: Oxford University Press, 1982. A symposium of twenty-two authors (in addition to court opinions and data tabulations). Four authors argue for and four against.

Berger, Raoul. *Death Penalties; The Supreme Court's Obstacle Course.* Cambridge, Mass.: Harvard University Press, 1982. A very densely argued lawyer's brief against the way the Supreme Court's constitutional interpretations were used to undercut existing death penalty laws.

Berns, Walter. *For Capital Punishment.* New York: Basic Books, 1979. Probably the best contemporary philosophical argument for the death penalty, on the grounds of the rightness of anger. "A moral community is not possible without anger and the moral indignation that accompanies it," (p. 156). Berns surveys very fairly "the case against," and argues strongly against the damage he feels to have been done by unwise penological views which value the rights of the accused above those of the community.

Black, Charles. *Capital Punishment: The Inevitability of Caprice and Mistake.* New York: W. W. Norton, 1974.

Block, Eugene B. *And May God Have Mercy . . .: The Case Against Capital Punishment.* San Francisco: Fearon, 1962. One journalist's encyclopedic argument, with extensive case material and a bibliography.

——. *When Men Play God: The Fallacy of Capital Punishment.* San Francisco: Cragmont Publications, 1983. A summary of the abolition argument, introduced by an analysis of the setbacks of the abolition cause since 1972. Includes updates on the rest of the world (pp. 97ff), specifically on Britain (pp. 143ff) and France (pp. 176ff).

Borchard, Edwin M. *Convicting the Innocent: Errors of Criminal Justice.* New Haven: Yale University Press, 1932. Borchard reviews in detail sixty-five cases of persons wrongly found guilty of crime. An introductory chapter analyzes how the errors came to be made and how they later came to light. To the reasons given by Frank (below), this adds cases where circumstantial evidence was added to perjury.

Bresnahan, James F., S. J., "Death as a Penalty in the United States of America." *New Concilium* 120 (December 1978). Survey of the contemporary American scene written for an international readership by a Catholic moral theologian who is also a lawyer.

Camus, Albert. "Reflections on the Guillotine." *Evergreen Review* 4:12 (March–April 1960): 1–58 (separate pagination); translated from the French (*La Nouvelle Revue Française*, June and July 1957). The existentialist novelist's testimony may be compared to that of Arthur Koestler in Great Britain.

Clark, Ramsey. "The Death Penalty and Reverence for Life." In *Crime in America*. New York: Simon and Schuster, 1970, 330ff. Author states that capital punishment corrupts the entire judiciary and correctional system.

Davis, John Jefferson. *Evangelical Ethics: Issues Facing the Church Today*. Philipsburg, N. J.: Presbyterian and Reformed Publishing Co., 1985. Davis surveys the historical, biblical, philosophical, and pragmatic issues surrounding capital punishment. He concludes that capital punishment is a very complex issue, but it "protects society from the hardened murderer and is an appropriate and fitting punishment for the most heinous of crimes." The death penalty is discussed on pp. 193–207.

Endres, Michael E. *The Morality of Capital Punishment*. Mystic, Conn.: Twenty-Third Publications, 1985. The author, a professor of criminal justice, Xavier University, Connecticut, surveys all of the humane and legal arguments.

Ezovsky, Gertrude. *Philosophical Perspectives on Punishment*. Albany: State University of New York Press, 1972.

Frank, Jerome, and Barbara Frank. *Not Guilty*. Garden City, N.Y.: Doubleday, 1957: thirty-six cases of innocent persons convicted. Judge Frank and Barbara Frank write that sometimes the cause of the mistake was an innocent error made by a witness. Other times the police or the prosecutor produced a false testimony by blackmail or a false confession by torture. Sometimes the rules of evidence or the legal help available deny the innocent a fair trial.

Geisler, Norman. *Christian Ethics: Options and Issues*. Grand Rapids, Mich.: Baker Book House, 1989. The author discusses capital punishment and its three major views (pp. 193–213). He surveys and then evaluates the rehabilitation view, the reconstruction view, and the retribution view.

Gerber, Rudolph J., and Patrick D. McAnany, eds. *Contemporary Punishment: Views, Explanations, and Justifications*. Notre Dame, Ind.: University of Notre Dame Press, 1972. A symposium bringing together philosophers, lawyers, social scientists, legislators, therapists, and a pope, discussing the four classical justifications for punishment: retribution, deterrence, social defense, and rehabilitation.

Glueck, Sheldon. *Crime and Correction*. Cambridge, Mass.: Addison-Wesley Press, 1952.

Gowers, Sir Ernest, chairman, 1953 Royal Commission report. A London psychiatrist said of report: "Never in the history of penological literature has such a devastating indictment of capital punishment been set before the public that is ultimately responsible for its maintenance." (See also Playfair and Sington, below, p. 267.)

Gray, Ian, and Moira Stanley. *A Punishment in Search of a Crime*. New York: Avon, 1989. Forty-two brief argumentative statements, all negative, many based on personal involvement.

Haas, Kenneth C., and James A. Inciardi, eds. *Challenging Capital Punishment: Legal and Social Science Approaches*, Vol. 24, Sage Criminal Justice System Annuals. Beverly Hills, Calif.: Sage Publications, 1988.

Hart, H. L. A. *Punishment and Responsibility: Essays in the Philosophy of Law*. New York: Oxford University Press, 1968.

Hoekema, David. "Capital Punishment: The Question of Justification." *Christianity Today* 96 (March 29, 1979), 338ff.

Joseph, Ingle, B. *Lat Rights: 13 Fatal Encounters with the State's Justice*. Nashville: Abingdon Press, 1990. A minister's autobiographical account of his ministry on death row.

Koestler, Arthur. *Reflections on Hanging* New York: Macmillan, 1957. Immigrant Englishman, novelist, social critic, "political tutor to his generation," Koestler synthesized the case against capital punishment in terms of the British scene in his time. His chapter "The Heritage of the Past" is the best easily available summary of the older history of capital punishment in the English tradition. His chapter "Doomed by Mistake" offers the British counterpart of the studies of Borchard and Frank. His preface to the American edition enriches his argument with strong contemporary case references.

Lawrence, Michael. *U. C. Davis Law Review*. 18, no. 4 (Summer 1985). Nineteen lawyers and social scientists in a symposium on the death penalty.

Lewis, Clive Staples. "The Humanitarian Theory of Punishment." In *God in the Dock*. Grand Rapids, Mich.: Eerdmans, 1970, 287–94, and "On Punishment: A Reply to Criticism," *ibid.*, 295–300. The famous Anglican apologist argues for a concept of desert whereby the reason for punishment must not be reduced either to social utility or to the individual's well-being.

McCafferty, James M. ed. *Capital Punishment*. New York: Aldine, 1972; Lieber-Atherton, 1973. A symposium of sixteen authors. Five advocate and six reject the death penalty. Hugo A. Bedau contributes to the volume a general factual survey concerning the recent history of legal reform in the U.S.A.

Meltsner, Michael. *Cruel and Unusual: The Supreme Court and Capital Punishment*. New York: Random House, 1973. Recounts the work of lawyers leading to the courts' striking down most laws authorizing capital punishment on the grounds that their application was unequal and capricious, thereby open to being racially discriminatory, and therefore constituting "cruel and unusual punishment" in the sense of the Eighth Amendment. This stopped executions (*Furman* v. *Georgia*, 1972) until states could prepare new legislation. The work was coordinated by the Legal Defense Fund.

Miller, Kent S., and Betty Davis Miller, *To Kill and Be Killed: Case Studies from Florida's Death Row*. Pasadena, Calif.: Hope Publishing House, 1989. Ten case histories, selected as representative of different issues. The authors believe that two of the ten were in fact innocent and that in most states four others would have been given a lesser punishment, on the ground of diminished capacity, and one as a juvenile.

Nathanson, Stephen. *An Eye for an Eye? The Morality of Punishing by Death*. Totowa, N.J.: Rowman and Littlefield, 1987. Review of the entire argument with the tools of academic philosophy. Demonstrates exceptionally well the complexity of notions like "deserving," "cruelty," and "vengeance."

Playfair, Giles, and Derrick Sington. *The Offenders: The Case Against Legal Vengeance*. New York: Simon and Schuster 1957. An attorney and a journalist recount seven cases of persons convicted of shocking offenses. Their evidence counts against the claim that the death penalty can be administered fairly or that it deters crime.

Rush, Benjamin. "An Enquiry Into the Effects of Public Punishments Upon Criminals, and Upon Society, 1787," and "Considerations on the Injustice and Impolicy of Punishing Murder by Death," 1972, reprinted in *Reform of Criminal Law in Pennsylvania: Selected Inquiries*

1787–1819. New York: Arno Press, 1972. Contemporary and friend of Benjamin Franklin, Benjamin Rush is counted as the first American to make the case against capital punishment on general grounds of social hygiene.

Tabak, Ronald J., and J. Mark Lane. "The Execution of Injustice: A Cost and Lack-of-Benefit Analysis of the Death Penalty." *Loyola of Los Angeles Law Review* 23, no. 1 (November 1989): 59–146. The fullest statement by lawyers of the case against the death penalty on the grounds of unfairness within the system.

van den Haag, Ernest, ed. *The Death Penalty: A Debate*. New York: Plenum, 1983. Van den Haag is a social philosopher; John P. Conrad is a criminologist at the Criminal Justice Center of Sam Houston State University. A thorough, good-mannered, yet hard-hitting debate across the full range of topics of moral and social philosophy.

Van Ness, Daniel W. *Crime and Its Victims*. Downers Grove, Ill.: InterVarsity Press, 1986.

Wenham, Gordon. "Law and the Legal System in the Old Testament." In *Law, Morality, and the Bible*. Bruce Kaye and Gordon Wenham, eds. Downers Grove, Ill.: InterVarsity Press, 1978, 24–52.

White, Welsh S. *The Death Penalty in the Eighties: An Examination of the Modern System of Capital Punishment*. Ann Arbor, Mich.: University of Michigan Press, 1987. An impartial lawyer's wide-ranging and detailed survey of how court decisions since the resumption of executions have modified the procedures and the outcomes of death penalty prosecution in the U.S.A.

Wright, Christopher T. H. *An Eye for an Eye: the Place of Old Testament Ethics Today*. Downers Grove, Ill.: InterVarsity Press, 1983. Despite the title, Wright does not deal carefully with the issue of equal retribution.

Zimring, Franklin E., and Gordon Hawkins. *Capital Punishment and the American Agenda.*. Cambridge: Cambridge University Press, 1986.

Index of Scripture References

A. The Old Testament

B. The New Testament

Index of Persons and Subjects

The Authors

H. Wayne House is academic dean and professor of theology at Westrn Baptist College, and current president aof the Evangelical Theological Society. He holds the M.A. in Biblical and Patristic Greek from Abilene Christian University, master's degrees in pastoral and biblical studies from Western Baptist Seminary, and doctorates from Concordia Seminary (St. Louis), and the O. W. Coburn School of Law.

Dr. House has written numerous articles for scholarly journals; he co-authored *The Christian Confronts His Culture* (Moody Press, 1983), and edited and contributed to *Restoring the Constitution. 1787—1987: Essays in Celebration of the Bicentennial* (Probe, 1987), and edited and contributed to the *Legal Handbook for Christian Ministries* (Baker, 1989). He also edited *Divorce and Remarriage: Four Christian Views* (InterVarsity Press, 1988) and is writing *Colossians and Philemon*, a forthcoming volume in the Wycliffe Commentary Series (Moody Press).

He and his wife Leta Frances McConnell have two children and reside in Salem, Oregon.

John Howard Yoder is professor of theology at the University of Notre Dame. He had served the Mennonite denomination in overseas relief and mission administration, in ecumenical relations, and in theological education, being president of Goshen Biblical Seminary.

Dr. Yoder is a graduate of the College of Wooster, Goshen College, and the University of Basel.

Dr. Yoder's best-known writings are *The Politics of Jesus* (Eerdmans, 1972) and *The Priestly Kingdom* (University of Notre Dame Press, 1984). He has also authored *The Original Revolution* (1971), *What Would You Do?* (1983), *He Came Preaching Peace* (1985), as well as other volumes all published by Herald Press. With H. Wayne Pipken, he translated and edited *Balthasar Hubmaier: Theologian of Antibaptism* (Herald Press, 1989).

Dr. Yoder and his wife Anne Marie Guth are the parents of six living children and reside in Elkhart, Indiana.